WHY POPULISTS ARE WINNING
and How to Beat Them

ALSO BY LIAM BYRNE

Turning to Face the East
Black Flag Down
Dragons
The Inequality of Wealth

WHY POPULISTS ARE WINNING
and How to Beat Them

Liam Byrne

An Apollo Book

First published in the UK in 2026 by Head of Zeus, Ltd
part of Bloomsbury Publishing Plc

Copyright © Liam Byrne, 2026

The moral right of Liam Byrne to be identified
as the author of this work has been asserted in accordance with
the Copyright, Designs and Patents Act of 1988.

All rights reserved. No part of this publication may be: i) reproduced
or transmitted in any form, electronic or mechanical, including photocopying,
recording or by means of any information storage or retrieval system without prior
permission in writing from the publishers; or ii) used or reproduced in any way for
the training, development or operation of artificial intelligence (AI) technologies,
including generative AI technologies. The rights holders expressly reserve this
publication from the text and data mining exception as per Article 4(3)
of the Digital Single Market Directive (EU) 2019/790.

9 7 5 3 1 2 4 6 8

A catalogue record for this book is available from the British Library.

ISBN (HB): 9781035920921
ISBN (ePub): 9781035920938

Printed and bound in Great Britain by Clays Ltd, Elcograf S.p.A.

Bloomsbury Publishing Plc
50 Bedford Square, London, WC1B 3DP, UK
Bloomsbury Publishing Ireland Limited,
29 Earlsfort Terrace, Dublin 2, D02 AY28, Ireland

HEAD OF ZEUS LTD
5–8 Hardwick Street
London, EC1R 4RG

To find out more about our authors and books
visit www.headofzeus.com
For product safety related questions contact productsafety@bloomsbury.com

To democrats, everywhere

Contents

1. The Age of Rage　　　　　　　　　1
2. Meet the Populists　　　　　　　　21
3. The End of Hope　　　　　　　　　43
4. What's the Message?　　　　　　　65
5. Magical Thinking　　　　　　　　　81
6. Engage and Enrage　　　　　　　　98
7. Follow the Money　　　　　　　　119
   Conclusion: How to Beat Them　　140

   Acknowledgements　　　　　　　　179
   Notes　　　　　　　　　　　　　　183

1

The Age of Rage

It was not a winter of discontent. It was a boiling summer. Up and down a sun-burnt England, the red-and-white flags of St George were cable-tied to lamp-posts in an angry campaign to 'raise the colours'. Outside nondescript hotels, riot police locked arms, struggling to hold the line against crowds hell-bent on storming shelters for asylum-seekers. And in the papers – papers that once prided themselves on nuance and judgement – editors recast bigotry as bravery and gave star billing to a woman convicted of urging the immolation of foreigners.

But 2025 wasn't just a British fever dream.

Across the Channel, France's far right marched with thousands to celebrate their strongest showing in a generation. In Germany, the far-right Alternative for Germany (AfD) muscled its way into second place in the polls. In Austria, a party founded by a former SS officer no longer skulked in the shadows – it was the largest force in parliament. From Rome to Budapest to Warsaw, nationalist movements were no longer shouting in the streets – they were taking office and wielding power. Meanwhile in Washington, the new President was ordering the National

Guard – complete with flak jackets and automatic weapons – onto the streets of the capital.

Some 2 billion people went to vote in 2024. It was democracy's biggest year. By the time the votes were counted, results declared and oaths of office sworn, one thing was crystal clear: populism had reached a new high-water mark. Yet is this peak populism? Or populism's tipping point? In the polls its parties are soaring. In the media, its myths are normalised. In office, its leaders have evolved from the political 'improv' of their early days in office to a well-defined political project.

All told, populists now lead one-quarter of the planet's democracies.[1] Authoritarian populists lead governments in Hungary, Italy and Slovakia and hold cabinet seats in six EU countries.[2] In nine more, they're either topping the polls or propping up ruling coalitions.[3] On 1 June 2024, Poland's Karol Nawrocki – backed by the populist Law and Justice Party – clinched the presidency by a razor-thin margin. In Britain's 2024 general election, Reform became the most electorally successful far-right formation in modern British history.[4] As I write this now in the House of Commons Library, Reform bests the Labour Party, the Liberal Democrats and the Conservatives in the polls. But no election was as consequential as the re-election of President Trump. When Donald Trump stormed back into the White House in 2024, he didn't ride a wave of admiration. He surfed a tide of fury. The Democrats, for all their data and dollars, failed to grasp the depth of American rage. And the populists won because he did.

The danger we must now confront is that populists could, and might, push through this tipping point: seizing the hard power of office and the soft power of the agenda across the West when history itself is turning. For the three great trends that created the politics of today – like waves racing into shore – are growing stronger. And the inevitable crisis, the trigger, may tip us into new and darker times.

Populism has the maddening quality of being easy to spot but hard to define. A bit like pornography, you know it when you see it. Political scientists like the simple, broad definition of Dutch scholar Cas Mudde. He describes populism as 'a thin-centred ideology that considers society to be ultimately separated into two homogeneous and antagonistic groups, "the pure people" versus "the corrupt elite"'. And politics, insist the populists, 'should be an expression of the *volonté générale* (general will) of the people'.[5]

Yet today's radical right-wing populists offer far more than this. They are authoritarian populists.[6] They advance an 'us v. them' politics thin in theory but in practice thick with menace: a stew of tribalism, nostalgia, nativism and authoritarianism stirred into a potent political project. It's soaked in the brandy of nostalgia with a saccharine appeal to a lost past. It combines a *cri de cœur* to 'restore the nation' in a 'moral panic' at what's billed as a civilisational struggle against elites within and foreigners without. Its appeal is a simple trick: to tell people their anger at a rigged system is justified – but then to redirect that anger towards a different target. Not just the elite but the outsider: the migrant, the minority. And the prescription? It is the prescription of every extremist down the ages; a strong man to stop the rot.

What populism is not, is new. The historian Eric Hobsbawm once described the nineteenth-century Luddites and their attacks on new industrial machines as 'collective bargaining by riot'.[7] Populism is something similar. It is what rebellion looks like in a democracy. That is why it has surfaced whenever democracies have faltered – from the Narodniks in tsarist Russia to the Chartists in Victorian Britain, to the People's Party on the American plains, to the Poujadists of post-war France. But modern authoritarian populism is different in one crucial respect: it rises not from a single grievance but from the crushing weight of economic disappointment and digital division combined with the cultural anxiety that comes with collapsing social trust and evaporating social capital. Which is why it has accelerated since the Great Financial Crisis, as three great trends – the great disillusion, the great division and the new age of human movement – have all grown stronger and stronger. Together these seismic forces have triggered an earthquake.

The great disillusion

First came the great disillusion. The global economy, built after the fall of the Berlin Wall, has handed extraordinary riches to a lucky few. Yet for billions it is now failing. Generation after generation is now worse off than its parents and grandparents. Disillusioned that anything might change, more are losing faith in the virtues of democracy.

The global financial crisis of 2008 was a watershed. Before it, populists struggled. After it, populists grew stronger. It is often said that populism gained appeal because voters 'blamed' elites for causing the crash. But in truth the real anger was with the failure to fix the aftermath. Too many governments offered austerity at home and drift abroad: a lost decade unfolded in which living standards flat-lined, the debt burdens grew heavier and hope drained away.[8]

Look at the figures. The Western promise was supposed to be that free societies grew faster. But that is not what's happened since 2010. In fact, between 2010 and 2025 the economies of the countries around the world counted as 'free' grew on average a fifth less than the countries classed as dictatorships.[9]

This great broken promise helps explain why old loyalties to the mainstream political parties, forged in the Big Bang of nineteenth-century democracy, had atrophied to mere weak affinities. The collapse of confidence is now so pronounced that turnout everywhere is in free-fall – governments find themselves 'ruling the void' where lively consent should flourish. And in the void, bitterness now boils.

I have seen it first hand. For the last 20 years, I've run residents' meetings and gazebo surgeries every month in my constituency in East Birmingham. In those church halls, community centres and on windy street corners, I've heard the anger rise like a pot coming to the boil; the chronic pressure on living standards, the loss of pride in place as decline sets in, the pessimism about the future, the sense of dispossession triggered by immigration – and above all the rage at broken politics.

The great division

These challenges would be difficult to manage at any time. But a second force now drives the tidal waves in politics.

Drama and democracy are as old as ancient Greece. They emerged together in Athens as essential companions. Drama showcased the conflicts and dilemmas of the day, from which democracy sought to find the reconciliations and compromise which might allow a community to live a good life and flourish. But today, the digital revolution has created vast new squares and boulevards online through which the angry now march and shout in a cacophony that roils the daily debate, frustrating efforts to 'meet in the middle' and renew the coherent amity on which democracy ultimately rests. And it is getting worse.

A decade ago, I visited Scotland Yard, where high up in the old towers was a long, hot, cavernous room that was home to one of Britain's most important teams fighting against extremism. The Counter Terrorism Internet Referral Unit (CTIRU) was a tiny team of young police officers tasked with taking down extremist content whenever and wherever it is found.

Sealed off behind heavy signal-jamming doors, the room looked like a call centre; crammed desks overloaded with gigantic computer screens over which hung laminated signs showing the insignia of the extremists marked out as the operators' targets. These young officers were the best of British policing: full of practical wisdom and good, old-fashioned common sense, blessed with bonhomie and determination, patriotic to the core. They felt like they were winning. But ten years on, the battle against online extremism is all but lost – and the result is a West even more divided than before.

In 2025, the Pew global survey found that on average 72 per cent of adults across 25 nations considered the spread of false information online as a major threat to their country.[10]

It's now the number-one threat cited in most major Western countries. So it is no surprise that data now onfirms that social trust has eroded sharply in America and remains deeply stratified by class, race and age across rich democracies. In survey after survey, younger, poorer and more precarious citizens are less likely to say that 'most people can be trusted'. And supporters of populist parties are the least trusting of all. Where trust drains and the ties between us weaken, so the restraints on extremism wither – and populism spreads.

Britain is not immune to this. Research from King's College London shows Brits believe the country is now more divided than at any time since tracking began.[11] Eighty-four per cent of the public say the country feels divided. The belief that we are split by 'culture wars' has shot up from 46 per cent in 2020 to 67 per cent in 2025. Half the public now believe British culture is changing too fast. Nearly half say the country was better in the past – and even young people are now nostalgic; almost a third of 16–24-year-olds agree that 'I would like my country to be the way it used to be'.

Someone who has studied this deeply is Professor Bobby Duffy, former research director at Ipsos MORI and now head of the Policy Institute at King's College. He explained the importance of these new findings: 'Rhetoric does seem to matter – and it's very clear that it has become more extreme. Views that would have been moderated and taken down from social-media platforms a year or two ago no longer are. There is increasingly solid academic evidence for what we can all see in our own experience of platforms and politics – that our information environment has become more extreme and divisive. And there is very solid evidence that exposure to those extreme views does shift individual attitudes and moves the social norm.'

Joined together, the Great Disillusion and the Great Division deepen the shock of the third great change of our era: the large-scale movement of people.

The new age of human movement

Nobody forgets their first visit to a refugee camp. As I walked through the Baharka camp in northwest Iraq, the air thick with dust and diesel, I looked out over the tents pitched in ragged lines. Amongst the ruin of lives, children did what children do everywhere. Little boys in wellies and flip-flops were pushing plastic trucks through the mud, building small worlds of their own. Their friends were chasing a half-flat football across a stony pitch, Barcelona FC tops hanging off narrow shoulders, while teenagers hung around inventing ways to fend off the boredom.

Here a young father, Ahmed, described what it was like carrying his five children through the mountains, all under nine. Refugee camps teach you some simple truths. Our indomitable will to survive will drive us to the most extraordinary extremes in search of the quiet miracle of a normal life – especially to keep our children safe, which is why half the residents of most camps are kids. Those who end up in camps are those who have lost literally everything. But those who can scrape together something – anything – will keep moving, by any means necessary.

Across the world, people are being driven from their homes by conflict, crushing poverty and climate change. According to the World Bank,[12] refugee numbers have doubled in a decade. But the much larger story is the economic migration driven by Western nations' need for labour. So while the *share* of migrants in the global population has remained relatively stable since 1960, *absolute numbers* have grown. In high-income countries, the World Bank reports, 'global migration increased more than three times faster than population growth'. In an age marked by division and frustration, a change of this magnitude could hardly fail to have a political consequence.

Things can only get better?

When I worked for Tony Blair in 1996, the campaign anthem was, famously, D:Ream's hit single 'Things Can Only Get Better'. I have now been in public life long enough to know that, however bad things are, they can always get worse. And if we look ahead, it is not hard to spot the risks that might take populism through the tipping point to control the mainstream, not because mainstream leaders are feeble, but because the storms are fierce. For these three great trends, the great disillusion, the great division and the the new age of movement, are unlikely to abate in the years to come. They will grow stronger.

The great disillusion may grow deeper as artificial intelligence wipes out millions of jobs. The IMF already warns that up to 60 per cent of jobs may be affected. Potentially half of advanced nations may experience reduced labour demand, downward pressure on wages or a jobs wipe-out,[13] which may accelerate countries' retreat into the beggar-thy-neighbour economics of the 1930s. The great division may grow deeper and more dangerous as social media grows its audience and new technology of AI-driven deep-fakes renders it finally impossible to discern fact from fiction. Meanwhile, human movement may accelerate. As the President of the World Bank often explains, over the next decade or two, some 1.2 billion young people are about to enter the labour market across emerging economies. But the best-case scenarios are that anywhere between 200 million and 600 million will be left without jobs. In the search for hope, many will move to the countries of Europe and America, where ageing societies urgently need younger workers to maintain their economic dynamism.

If they are badly managed, these long-running trends will provide populists with plenty of firewood. But in politics, you need a real crisis to truly change the political weather. An economic crisis, like a financial meltdown from which the now debt-laden West may lack the capacity to respond, could enable populists to seize even more power. This is no fanciful scenario. It's the expectation of many in the markets.

The trigger

The famous Beaux-Arts façade of the New York Stock Exchange looks out not onto Wall Street but Broad Street. With its Corinthian columns, its Greek pediment crowded with allegorical figures, its huge American flags stirring in the canyoned light, it is a modern temple built with marble calm to reassure a risky business. But step inside and you're hit with a flash-bang charge of testosterone, adrenaline and data.

On the spotless, bustling trading floor – a grand arena lit like a film set – banks of screens crowd the space. Numbers, news and logos race across walls of digital colour while live TV commentators in their broadcast booths mix with traders buying and selling stocks and stories.

I arrived one Friday afternoon – 17 May 2024, to be precise – with my committee for a tour. As five o'clock approached, we gathered beneath the balcony of the NYSE Board Room, where on its perch was the brass bell that rings out the end of the trading week. We could feel the anticipation rise. The bell sounded with a bright clang that cut through the noise. Up went the cheers. Applause rolled across the floor. And then the number flashed: the Dow Jones had closed above 40,000 for the first time in history – 40,003.59. The mood was buoyant, almost oblivious. Whatever storms were gathering, Wall Street had hit a record. The market has been rising ever since. Which is exactly why some people are getting very worried.

Markets tend to crash when everyone is happy to think nothing can go wrong. In 1929, Wall Street believed the party could last for ever. In 2008, the banks convinced themselves that housing prices would only ever go up – until the bubble burst. Today, markets seem convinced that once again 'this time it is different' and the dizzying advance of new technology justifies the exuberance that is sending indexes to new heights. In fact we stand once more on the edge of a precipice. Why? Because the bond between economic rationality and political rationality has broken.

The chief executive of one major bourse explained it to me like this: once upon a time, he said, 'the markets felt very comfortable ... what was economically rational behaviour was often the politically rational choice to make. That is no longer the case'. Brexit, Trump, tariffs – each revealed that politics now bends away from economics – just at the moment when the era of falling interest rates comes to an end. For three decades, cheap money has underpinned housing booms, private equity, and market exuberance. But now Washington is running vast fiscal deficits while enforcing tariffs. Warming to his theme, my Cassandra warned me that these were all ideas which 'will hurt productivity, will hurt margins and will hurt growth'.

Today, although America provides perhaps a fifth of global economic output, its stock market makes up three-quarters of the value of the world's equity investment in companies. Yet there is simply no iron law that America's dominance will last for ever. After all, the Japanese stock exchange once made up 40 per cent of global equity values. Today, it is 5 per cent. Capital flows can collapse overnight. But if that happens to the New York Stock Exchange, we risk an economic shock like that which followed the Wall Street crash: unemployment up, desperation up and extremists carried into office on a tidal wave of rage.

And this is not a moment in our history when we want populists controlling the levers of power, for the simple reason that too many bring their nasty habits to the table: an unholy trinity of appeasement, autocracy and avarice. To understand this better, I had to go back to school.

Appeasement, autocracy and avarice

St Antony's College, Oxford was founded in the uneasy peace after the Second World War and acquired a reputation as 'the spy college' – a place where soldiers, diplomats and scholars studied how the world worked and how it might be remade. Le Carré even imagined one of George Smiley's agents as a former student. The myth endured because it carried a kernel of truth.

It was here, in 2025, that I took up a parliamentary fellowship and joined a Conservative colleague, John Glen – another former chief secretary to the Treasury – to convene a series of packed-out lectures on how to solve difficult problems in an age of polarisation. Over four months, what I heard from some of Britain's most experienced figures in security and intelligence, development and diplomacy was a warning: populist politics is dangerous in general. It is uniquely dangerous in the times in which we now find ourselves.

Appeasement?

'This is', ventured a former head of the Royal College of Defence Studies, 'a once-in-a-five-hundred-year moment.' The long hegemony of the West is giving way to a multipolar world in which China is not just a military rival but an administrative, industrial and demographic superpower. Comparing the dangers of today to the 1980s, a former head of the Secret Intelligence Service put it starkly: 'Back then we lived with the shadow of annihilation. Today the world is more even – America no longer dominates, China has risen, India is emerging, and Europe is in relative decline. That makes for greater competition, more manoeuvring and more disruption.'

Nuclear proliferation, once contained, now spreads. New technologies from AI to hypersonics are remaking the art and arsenal of power. The 'rules-based system' is fraying into a messy, networked world where authoritarian leaders concentrate power, and kleptocrats manipulate connections that stretch across continents. And at the very moment allies look to Washington for steadiness, President Trump is radically recalibrating America's role in the multilateral system it built. It is not quite an 'Amexit', but it demands much more from the rest of us – not least in standing up to a Russia willing, like the Nazis in 1930s Spain, to seize land, terrorise civilians and bomb the infrastructure on which daily life depends.

Yet too often, we can find populists cosying up to Moscow. In November 2025, the former leader of Reform UK in Wales was sentenced to over a decade in jail after admitting taking bribes for pro-Russia interviews and speeches.

Worse, the populists' hunger for division is dangerous; they cannot build the unity at home or the alliances abroad that the times now require. Their divisive style corrodes the trust on which collective security depends. At home, our best defence is what is now known as a 'whole-of-society' approach – a Finnish-style unity of purpose in which a nation locks together to defend itself. As one former RAF leader remarked, 'The Finns can field 285,000 troops tonight. That's what national unity looks like.'

Abroad, a similar mindset is essential. As Professor Ngaire Woods reminded us, even when a hegemon like the United States steps back, smaller states can still forge institutions strong enough to restrain chaos – but only if partners trust that agreements will endure beyond a single election cycle. Populists shatter that trust. In their world of 'punch-you-in-the-face' deal-making, commitments snap, continuity dies and the ropes that bind old allies together fray. So, unless we resist the populists' siren calls of tribalism, we risk being beaten without a shot fired, not least because populism is so expensive.

Autocracy – and its expense

The second great risk of populism is autocracy – and its economic cost. There are now enough populists in power for us to see the pattern clearly. The strongman sits at the heart of authoritarian populism, whether in Erdoğan's Turkey, Orbán's Hungary, Duterte's Philippines or Trump's America. Populism calls itself a people's crusade, yet in practice it is run by a narrow, jealous clique. Having divided a nation to gain office, they set about dividing its institutions to keep it: attacking the media, undermining elections, browbeating judges, intimidating civil servants, denigrating scientists and deriding constitutions, courts and international organisations as 'fake news', 'the deep state', 'a swamp' or 'a talking club'.

But when populists tear down the fences around executive power, they threaten what Daron Acemoglu and James Robinson call the Narrow Corridor[14] – the precious zone within which modern liberty evolved – the liberty that was so essential for modern economic growth. In that corridor, the state is strong enough to keep order, yet 'shackled' by norms, institutions and an active citizenry. Populists cut those shackles. They centralise power in the leader. And once those fetters break, the risks multiply: the most extreme danger is of a Weimar-style collapse of institutions; but a more common risk in the short run is economic damage, swift and severe.[15]

How severe? In an economic study of a century of 51 populist governments,[16] economists found that after 15 years of populist leadership, real GDP per head is more than 10 per cent lower. Populists buy applause on credit: a sugar-rush of giveaways financed by borrowing. Debts swell, inflation rises and, as judicial independence erodes and property rights weaken, investment withers. Autocratic leaders cannot resist meddling in the economy with such unpredictability that the confidence to take risks evaporates, and as Federal Reserve governor Lisa Cook once warned, uncertainty is a tax.

What would this mean for Britain? A lost fortune. A one-percentage-point growth penalty every year is devastating. It would mean almost £4,700 lost per person by the mid-2030s – around £22,000 per head over the decade. Autocracy economics is expensive. Populists promise prosperity. They deliver penury. Of course, not for themselves.

Avarice

The third tragedy of populism is avarice. Populists campaign on enriching the people, yet once in office they spend an extraordinary amount of time enriching themselves. Avarice puts its feet up on the desk. And the kleptosphere – that dark, sprawling zone of shell companies, hidden trusts and anonymous wealth – metastasises through a system we in the West helped to build: the Cayman Islands; the British Virgin Islands; the anonymous companies and secretive trusts. These were not inventions of Moscow or Beijing; they were invented in London and New York. And into these systems flow the spoils of stolen states.

Anne Applebaum, one of the world's leading experts on modern kleptocracy, has mapped this system in forensic detail. When I asked her how far populists had sunk, she was not short of examples.

Take Viktor Orbán, a leader alleged to have taken European money meant for his people and lent it to his friends. 'Orbán set up this system of stealing EU money,' she explained, 'diverting EU funding that went to companies close to him.' It was not an original model, Anne continued: 'he created the equivalent of the Russian oligarchs in Hungary. He just followed the same pattern.' A childhood neighbour, his son-in-law, his father – all were turned into businessmen by the stroke of state power and endowed with a network of companies, dependent on the government, that also just happened to control most of the country's media.

This is populism as a business model: a cartel stitched together by patronage and propaganda. And Hungary is not alone. Applebaum points to Poland's Law and Justice Party creating its own oligarchs; Austria's Freedom Party caught plotting to capture companies; French far-right leaders repeatedly indicted for misuse of public funds. The conclusion is inescapable. Populism may rage against elites but it feathers its own nests. It does not drain the swamp – it digs it deeper. Populist politics is too often not public service but plunder. Not democracy but deals without ideals.

History's warning

History is rich in warnings for today. The rhymes between our moment and the late 1920s are not hard to miss. By

1927, the West had survived the Great War, the Spanish flu and the ruinous inflation of the post-war years. What dawned was a golden day for some. Stock markets boomed, gilding fortunes for a lucky few. For millions more, new marvels – electrification, radio, motor cars – transformed daily life.

Yet behind the bright lights, darker currents stirred. It was, as historian Richard Overy observed, a 'morbid age', haunted by a 'presentiment of pending disaster', gripped by the fear that 'our way of life' was in mortal peril. Intellectuals drafted obituaries for capitalism. Eugenicists filled halls with talk of 'race suicide'. Millions marched to defend the League of Nations and plead for peace.[17]

Within two years the Wall Street crash ripped through Western economies. The Great Depression bit. Unemployment soared. Peace unravelled. And in the crisis, two nations took two very different paths. Economic catastrophe is the great accelerator of extremism. As historian Richard Evans has shown, Weimar Germany might have muddled through its chronic weaknesses. '[I]t would need a catastrophe of major dimensions,' he wrote, 'if an extremist party like the Nazis was to gain mass support. [But] in 1929, with the sudden collapse of the economy in the wake of the Stock Exchange crash in New York, it came.'[18]

By 1931, one in three German workers was unemployed. Young men drifted listlessly on Berlin's trains. The jobless and their dependents made up a fifth of the entire population. Families put off marriages and children. The Depression, Evans concludes, 'pushed [the Republic] beyond the point of no return'.[19] By 1933, the Nazis had taken office.

Reflecting on what the defenders of democracy got wrong, historian Christian Goeschel offered me a stark verdict. They 'should have been more courageous. They should have been so much more courageous in promoting the Weimar Republic.' Instead, timidity became systemic. 'They were basically tiptoeing. They thought, should we do this? Should we do that?' Robust defence of liberalism, he concluded, cannot be left to legal process or half-measures. It must be fought for boldly – or it will be lost.

I emphatically do not believe that we risk a repeat of the extremism of the 1930s, with all that followed. Not least because I believe we can learn from the alternative path created by a politician who showed how a crisis can be properly met: Franklin Roosevelt.

Renewing the radical centre

The purpose of this book is simple: to explain why populists are winning and to set out the beginnings of a project to beat them. At its heart is a single ambition – to reclaim and renew the radical centre of our politics. Not as a party label, but as a political, economic and moral project: realistic about money, radical about power, and rooted in the oldest democratic truth, that freedom grows as the bonds between us grow stronger, neighbour to neighbour and citizen to citizen. When cooperation is enlarged, so possibilities enlarge. When possibilities grow, so real freedom – our agency, options and opportunities - expands.

Renewing the radical centre begins with honesty. Not ignoring the anger that is obvious. Not soothing people with dull PowerPoints or denial. Renewal begins by recognising that the deep forces driving populism – the disillusion, the division, the disruption – will grow stronger unless they are met with a project as bold as Roosevelt's New Deal.

Over the past year of research, interviews and polling across Britain and beyond, a project to conquer populism has emerged. It is the outlines of a Rooseveltian renewal: a new deal for the age of AI, algorithmic anger and democratic fatigue. In the chapters ahead, I set out that plan – how we build a heroic coalition of common sense, restore fairness, rebuild opportunity, renew belonging and create a state that performs with integrity and pride. Above all, it is a vision for how we revive a patriotism anchored not in exclusion but in our best ideals: decency, duty, fairness and freedom.

History offers us a blunt warning. In Weimar, democracy died when its defenders lost their nerve. In Roosevelt's America, it lived because they found their courage. If we do not fight to renew democracy, history shows what follows. If we fight with courage, history shows what's possible. Mainstream politics must recognise and ride the tide of anger that powers the populist rise, and rebuild the radical centre of Western liberalism. Mainstream leaders cannot take shelter from the storm. They must sail the tempest.

2

Meet the Populists

After the drama of an election campaign comes the banality of counting votes. Exhausting weeks are spent slogging it out on the doorsteps, online and on the airwaves, writing and delivering leaflets and direct mail, filming little videos, knocking on doors and checking where to find your voters – punctuated just occasionally by actually making a speech or two.

Campaigns restore your faith in the judgement of your fellow citizens. They have a sixth sense about where the country needs to go. Most are more than pleasant when you interrupt their tea. You learn to avoid those nasty, rusty letterboxes that scrape the skin off the back of your hand when you push your leaflets through. But your feet get sore, the days blur into one long mental miasma and you start dreaming about imaginary conversations. And then, just as you reach your last reserves, it's all over. A wave of relief. You retreat for junk food, a stiff drink, a hot bath. Then it's off to a municipal hall, where the ballot boxes are ferried, emptied, their contents counted and your fate sealed.

Counting votes takes a bewilderingly long time. I suppose that is probably a good thing. First the ballots are 'reconciled', checked and re-checked to make sure the votes in the box match the papers issued. Then the little slips are sorted, the spoilt ballots decorated with insults or rude drawings are put aside for a hard look if the race is tight. Finally, the votes for each candidate are bundled with elastic bands and stacked into neat piles by tellers working through the night and into the dawn. I've won elections by landslides and by the narrowest of margins. Through the stress and the euphoria I've never lost my admiration for the quiet, methodical wonder of the bureaucracy of democracy that helps settle a nation's future.

Yet over the years one thing has become impossible to miss: there simply aren't as many votes as there used to be. And that shrinking pile of ballot papers has one big implication. Populists are not sweeping to power on great waves of new support. They are advancing in an age of thinner turnouts, looser loyalties and more fragmented party systems. In a landscape where fewer people vote and more parties compete for their ballots, even modest surges of support can carry outsized political weight.

To grasp why populists are winning – and how to beat them – we must begin with two steps; first, we must understand the system in which they are competing: a system where lower participation and higher polarisation changes the arithmetic of victory. But second, we must look closely at populist voters themselves. And here the picture is getting clearer. Populist supporters remain smaller in number than their noise suggests. They are more polarised, more detached from the old party loyalties that once anchored political identity, and overwhelmingly rooted on the right: less qualified, more culturally conservative and more rooted in place. And in Britain, at least, this electorate appears divided into five distinct tribes – united in anger, but split by worldview. Among them are voters who can still be persuaded back to the mainstream. That is where hope lies.

Ruling the void?[1]

The irony of populism is that a movement that claims to speak for 'the people' rarely wins a majority of the population. Presidential victories in Hungary, Poland and even the United States look like exceptions but in fact they prove the rule. Even President Trump only secured 31 per cent of registered voters in 2024.

So how do populists win when the vast majority of people are moderate in temperament? Because the threshold for victory has fallen. Turnout is lower. Polarisation is higher. In these conditions you can win office – or seize a seat at the Cabinet table – with 15–30 per cent of voters.[2] When people walk away from the polling station, populists stride into power.

Turnout has been falling for decades.[3] Participation once rose steadily in countries like Germany, France and Italy, but since the 1980s it has fallen sharply almost everywhere. In 1945, more than eight in ten citizens voted in established democracies. Today the figure is closer to seven in ten. Turnout in Britain has drifted down to a percentage in the mid-60s. The United States languishes far lower still. Western leaders are often, in the words of political scientist Peter Mair, 'ruling the void' – governing populations that no longer believe the ballot box is a place to resolve their grievances.

But turnout is only half the story. The second shift is just as profound: electorates are now unmoored from the old loyalties that once organised political life. Votes now scatter across a wider cast of parties.

For much of the twentieth century, you knew your political tribe: you were Labour or Tory, Democrat or Republican, often because your parents were. Those anchors have snapped. The broad churches are emptying.

Nor are today's divides simply between left and right. They are between the polling station and the placard. Rather than vote, more now protest. Protest movements – from America's Occupy Wall Street to France's Gilets Jaunes to Britain's Extinction Rebellion – have become the new parliament of the disenchanted.

New parties and political entrepreneurs deepen the fractures. Analysing 300 elections since 1948, Thomas Piketty and his colleagues found that while anti-immigration parties have converged on traditional conservative economic ideas,[4] sociocultural polarisation has dramatically risen.[5] The result is an arms race of extremism. As Ezra Klein warns: 'To appeal to a yet more polarised public, institutions must polarise further; when faced with yet more polarised institutions, the public polarises further.'[6]

Hence, most Americans now say their politics is deeply divided.[7] Pew's 2022 study found 'strong or very strong disagreements' between supporters of different parties – and a sharp rise in the number of people who noticed this from the previous year.[8] This has transformed the outlook for mainstream politics. The Tony Blair Institute has found that support for predominant mainstream parties has fallen from three-quarters of votes in 2000 to just over half today.[9] The insurgent right now commands an average 10 per cent of the vote[10] – almost as much as the established right.[11]

These new shifts within old systems make a difference. Presidential election systems will often force candidates to actually secure 50 per cent of people who show up to vote. Most parliamentary systems do not. When votes fragment across more parties, each commands a smaller share – and the winning line drops. Lower turnout. Higher fragmentation. These are the conditions in which populists can triumph on a far smaller share of the electorate.

But understanding the system is only half the story. We must now turn to the people casting those votes. By and large, they are voters of the right.

Revolt on the right

In 1935, the journalist George Dangerfield wrote an exquisite obituary of the once-great British Liberal Party. Liberalism, he said, had long survived 'the destructive contradictions of daily reality by an almost mystical communion with the doctrine of laissez-faire and a profound belief in the English virtue of compromise'.[12] But its leadership, as muddled as its principles, could neither reconcile nor ride the chaotic forces of the early twentieth century: suffragettes, Irish Unionists, militant trade unionists, the rise of class politics.

Today, Dangerfield would write a different book: *The Strange Death of Tory England*.[13] For there is a simple truth about the rise of Reform UK. Its voters are overwhelmingly Conservatives.

To explore this, I invited Professor Jane Green, director of the authoritative British Election Study to brief a slightly nervous audience of Labour MPs. In a packed Room O in Portcullis House at the House of Commons, with its lovely views over Winston Churchill's statue in Parliament Square, Jane explained what was happening to Churchill's party.

'The most fundamental thing to understand', she said 'is that Reform voters are overwhelmingly disillusioned Tories.'

The pattern is not uniquely British. In 2024, 85 per cent of President Trump's 2020 voters backed him again.[14] In the UK, the numbers are just as stark and strategically important. More than 70 per cent of those who voted Reform in 2024 voted Conservative in 2019.[15] Three-quarters (74 per cent) of 2024 Reform voters have not voted Labour for approximately 20 years.[16]

Other research tells the same story. Campaign group 38 Degrees found 92 per cent of their Reform-minded members viewed Labour 'very unfavourably'.[17] Persuasion UK describes these people as historically anti-Labour voters who have cycled between voting Conservative, UKIP, non-voting or even Liberal Democrat. 'We should think of the vast majority of Reform voters', they explained to MPs 'as historically anti-Labour voters who are simply not, and seemingly never have been, in the Labour electoral universe.'[18]

The deeper logic, Jane explained, is this: 'The Brexit realignment has not disappeared – it has hardened into two blocks.' There is very little switching between the blocks but, within them, Reform is eating the Conservatives' lunch. As Jane put it: 'Labour doesn't have a Reform problem because it's losing votes – it has a Reform problem because it's not gaining them.'

Reform has captured the lion's share of Tory collapse and crucially now blocks disillusioned right-wing voters from defecting to the left by offering an alternative home on the right.

Which brings us to the question: what kind of Conservatives are they?

Less qualified, culturally conservative and rooted in place

To understand today's populist electorate, we must look beyond parties and into the deeper realignment reshaping politics across the West – a realignment of culture, class and place which explains why, although populists draw overwhelmingly from the right, the few voters drifting across the old left–right divide tend to be working-class, leave school earlier and are more economically insecure.

After President Trump's first election, Pippa Norris and Ronald Inglehart argued that the great trends reshaping Western progress – the feminisation of work, secularisation, diversity and the higher-education revolution – had triggered a cultural backlash among 'the inter-war generation, non-college graduates, [and] the working class'. These voters felt their values and beliefs were in jeopardy in the new world taking shape around them. Norris and Inglehart's research found Trump's support concentrated among older white men, small-town residents and those endorsing authoritarian values.[19]

But the more nuanced story comes from Thomas Piketty and colleagues,[20] who show that education has now become the defining political cleavage of our age. Graduates – who Piketty christens the 'Brahmin Left' – increasingly support progressive parties. Non-graduates – the 'Merchant Right' – increasingly support conservative and populist movements. This latter group is exposed to the vicissitudes of the new global economy. As economist Dani Rodrik explains, Obama–Trump switchers in 2016 showed not only greater racial hostility, but more economic insecurity, and negativity about both trade and immigration.[21]

Data from the last US elections confirms the insight. Since the high-water mark of the Obama years, Democrats have haemorrhaged support among non-white working-class voters – a collapse of roughly 30 points. Education is the underlying explanation. In 2024, Kamala Harris improved on Biden's performance with just one group: white college graduates. The Democrats won just one of the 29 states where fewer than 35 per cent of adults had a degree – but won all of the twelve states boasting populations where more than 40 per cent had gone to university.

Across Europe, the pattern is similar.[22] Voters for anti-immigration parties tend to be lower-income, less-qualified, more sceptical of institutions and supportive of strong-man leadership.[23] In Germany in 2024, the SPD lost almost a fifth of its vote to the AfD, which secured 38 per cent of blue-collar workers – more than three times the SPD's share. In Britain, the trend has been neatly explained by author David Goodhart as a tension between the Anywheres – mobile, university-educated, socially liberal – and the Somewheres: rooted in place, tied to community, and increasingly alienated from a political class they see as composed of liberal graduates. The 'Somewheres' are changing the way they vote, Goodhart told me, for a simple reason: 'The business and finance elite has partially deserted them. And their historic party has deserted them too – because you're all liberal graduates, the Brahmin wing of the Anywhere class.'

Taken together, these forces have forged a populist electorate that is:

- overwhelmingly drawn from the right
- more economically insecure
- more culturally conservative
- more rooted in place
- less qualified

These are the broad contours. But to truly understand why populists are winning, we must penetrate the mask of averages and make a closer study not of the general but of the specific: the five distinct tribes of populist voters. Let's meet them.

Populism's tribes

George Orwell once said that 'the gentleness of the English civilisation is perhaps its most marked characteristic'.[24] Doomscroll social media today and that is not how it feels, especially if you read the comments of those professing an affection for populist tropes.

To really understand populist voters we need to get into peoples' lives. Here I have the advantage of serving a constituency where many are tempted by Reform. I know their lives, their reasons, their rage. But to give this some analytical rigour, I teamed up with Best for Britain, Professor Bobby Duffy at the Policy Institute at King's College London, and pollsters YouGov. Together we designed one of the most detailed studies yet of Britain's new populist right: a nationally representative survey of 4,000 adults, alongside a parallel survey of 4,000 Reform supporters and considerers. We tested attitudes to politics, economics and identity and drew extensively on a parallel ethnographic study by research agency Faster Horses, which explored in depth how populist voters see their lives and their country.[25]

What emerged was a simple truth: populist voters are not one army marching under a single banner, but five distinct tribes. Two groups – which we christened the Melancholy Middle and Civic Pragmatists – are most open to persuasion. One – the Traditional Conservatives – is closest to the Tory tradition. Two more – Disgusted Disruptors and Left-Behind Collectivists – are anchored firmly in the populist right.

One obvious truth emerges from this summary: progressives should not set their message for hard-boiled groups, but for the voters who can actually be persuaded. Understanding these differences is essential for any serious strategy to rebuild trust, reconnect with the disaffected and renew the democratic centre because – and this is the crucial point – although all of these groups are considering voting Reform, analysis suggests that many amongst the Melancholy Middle and the Civic Pragmatists, which make up 40 per cent of the Reform-considering coalition, can be persuaded to change their minds, leave Reform and return to mainstream parties.

Their voting record, the issues they prioritise and their beliefs situate them closer to progressive parties, and sizeable minorities of both these groups would at least consider voting for the Conservatives, Labour, the Lib Dems or the Greens.

So who are the tribes of Reform? *

1. *The Disgusted Disruptors: fury of the forgotten*

The angriest of the populist right are the Disgusted Disruptors, about one in five potential Reform voters. They are also the most committed: 91 per cent say they fully intend to vote Reform, with only 9 per cent still merely considering it. Around 55 per cent are men, two-thirds are over 50, and almost a third are over 65. A quarter say they are struggling financially, and only just over a quarter (29 per cent) feel comfortable. Education levels are low to middling: 84 per cent have low or medium qualifications; just 16 per cent, high.

Think of the man you meet on the edge of a forgotten estate, late fifties, shoulders hunched against a future he no longer believes in. He tells you, almost flatly, that life 'is probably going to get worse', the way a doctor might deliver a terminal diagnosis. He once worked on the shop floor, did everything asked of him and now spends nights tumbling down YouTube rabbit holes that confirm his darkest fears.

---

* The statistics in this section can be found online, here: https://www.bestforbritain.org/decoding-populism-who-are-reform-uk-voters

Life has been hard. Work, once the measure of worth, now feels almost futile. Hope has leaked away. What remains is a brittle kind of fatalism, a belief that nothing can be fixed and no one will come. 'It's just looking bleaker and bleaker as a future of our country,' said a 43-year-old from Manchester. 'There's probably not a week that don't go by where I think I'd be better off outside of this country than inside of it.'

This group is consumed by the conviction that Britain has gone to the dogs. Immigration infuriates them. 'Wokeness' bewilders them. Brussels remains the ultimate betrayal. 'I do worry now, especially for my children and my grandchildren,' said a 66-year-old woman from Wolverhampton. 'It is a scary time and it's a scary world and it's a scary country.' They look at their town centres and see 'rows of shops boarded up ... all there seems to be now is vape shops or barbers, which look like they're some sort of front for organised crime,' as one 57-year-old from Stockport put it.

Their anger at politics is incandescent. They feel the country is slipping and no one – least of all our politicians – has a grip. Faith in authority – government, media, experts – has long since gone. Many admire Trump's defiance and binge-watch online influencers railing against elites who 'don't get it'. 'Our current crop of politicians', one man in his fifties told the Faster Horses study, 'are the most self-serving bunch of corrupt hypocrites ... completely detached from society.' They no longer expect politicians to fix things. They want someone to smash the system that failed them. Their politics is protest not policy. Mainstream parties will struggle to win back this group.

The more realistic question is whether they will bother to vote at all.

2. The Left-Behind Collectivists: believers in a social contract, now broken

The Left-Behind Collectivists are the next most loyal to Reform – about one in four potential Reform voters. Around 60 per cent are men, and again roughly two-thirds are in their fifties or older. Financially they are worse off than the Disgusted Disruptors: 34 per cent say they are struggling and just over a quarter say they're comfortable. They are less qualified: around 85 per cent have low or medium qualifications.

Picture a mid-fifties woman in NHS scrubs, walking home under a broken streetlight. She has spent a lifetime doing the right thing – working hard, raising a family, keeping faith with a country she believed would keep faith with her.

Now the bills pile up, her pension pot looks small, and she wonders where the good years went. 'We work all our lives and we've got so little to show for it,' she tells us, voice cracking with tired anger. She isn't cruel – her heart breaks for the neighbour relying on the food bank – but she cannot fathom why the state she served so long can no longer look after its own.

'I don't feel that life has gone the way I wanted it,' said a 47-year-old woman from Swansea. 'Growing up I had a lot of ambitions but over the years responsibilities of owning a home, paying bills, looking after a child, they've gotten in the way ... my focus has changed from thriving to just coping and making ends meet.'

They have kept calm and carried on through austerity, Covid and the cost-of-living crisis – yet still cannot get ahead. 'I'm fucking fuming, actually,' said a 54-year-old from Manchester. 'I've worked since the age of 14 ... but I don't seem to be getting anywhere because my money, my tax and insurance is going to the wrong people.'

They resent a system they see as stacked against them: taxes up, bills soaring, services cut, while 'the country's letting in thousands who take out more than they put in'. They are not libertarians. They are believers in a social contract but feel it has been betrayed – they are defenders of the NHS and social security, but convinced others are gaming the system. 'Talking about society today, it's very, very unequal,' said a 60-year-old from Bristol. 'People that have money can jump queues ... people who have worked hard ... are struggling. And that is just to buy basics, that's just to survive.'

They feel abandoned by politics. 'The politicians that run our country now, I don't feel connected to them,' said the woman from Swansea. 'They'll never worry about the bills. They'll never worry about how emotionally draining it is.' The result is a deep bitterness. 'It's quite soul-destroying to think I've become this bitter through no fault of my own,' said the woman from Manchester. 'I'd love to be in Parliament just for one day to make them realise how bad the state of this country has become.'

They want fairness restored, not chaos unleashed. Populists connect with their frustration. Progressives could still reach them with empathy and delivery. But

Left-Behind Collectivists need proof, not promises, that politics can again make work pay and decency count.

3. The Traditional Conservatives: the former Tory heartland

The Traditional Conservatives are believers in thrift, duty, order and the quiet pride of self-reliance. They are a relatively small proportion – about one in seven – of potential Reform voters, and nearly four-fifths say they are intending to vote that way.

They are the oldest tribe: almost three-quarters are over 50 and around 60 per cent are men. They often left school young (though around a fifth have a high level of education), learned a trade and built a modest prosperity with decades of hard graft. Now retired or semi-retired, they enjoy the fruits of effort – a pension, a home, perhaps a caravan holiday abroad. You'll find them on golf courses and in garden centres, men and women who built small businesses from nothing and still carry the pride of a job well done. They say it plainly: 'I make my own way.' They're not bitter – just exasperated. They are also the most financially secure: 51 per cent say they are comfortable and less than one in ten are struggling.

They remember a time when Britain felt orderly, adult, competent. Now the high street is hollowed out, the borders feel porous, and ministers look like children playing dress-up. They're not extremists; they simply want the country run with the same common sense they applied to their trades.

'I've worked hard all my life, never been unemployed,' said a 54-year-old from Birmingham. 'I'm responsible for my own life.' They watch the news with disbelief. Britain, they think, has lost its backbone. Too much debt. Too many handouts. Too little common sense. 'My main concern is my children and my grandchildren's future,' a 71-year-old from Birmingham told us. 'Can this country sustain itself in its present form? The answer is no.'

They are loyal to the flag and sceptical of Brussels. Immigration and social change feed their sense of a nation going backwards. 'Immigration ... is destabilising the country,' one man said. 'There is a lot of wrongdoers coming across ... living in hotels, getting benefits galore ... the cost of it is impacting services we should take for granted.' Their anger is tinged with weary resignation: 'The world today, it's not a very good place ... everything's going backward, until we get a leader that will lead and not just sit on the fence.'

Many once voted Conservative and some could once again if they sensed a return of competence. Their politics is nostalgic rather than nihilistic: they want a steady hand, not a wrecking ball. But for now, Reform speaks more plainly to their exasperation than the party they once called their own.

4. *The Melancholy Middle: still coping, no longer confident*

The Melancholy Middle are Britain's uneasy mainstream: about one in five potential Reform voters, almost perfectly gender-balanced. Politically, they are less locked in: 60 per cent say they intend to vote Reform, but a substantial 40 per cent are only 'considering'. They are much more open to Labour, Lib Dems and Greens than those among the first three tribes.

These are the soft-spoken souls of England's market towns, people who moved for quiet streets and greenery only to watch their local high street decay. In fact, they see decline everywhere: rising crime and an economy that no longer rewards effort. Their local pride is bruised. 'This town has got so much history,' one woman told us. 'It's been shit on from a great height.' She would not walk down the high street alone at night.

They are spread across the life course though over half are over 50, and a third are over 65. Financially, they sit in the middle: 41 per cent place themselves in the 'middle' band, 44 per cent feel comfortable, and 14 per cent are struggling. On paper, they are doing okay – earning around £35,000–39,000 a year, with nearly half saying they are coping well – but the optimism that once fuelled their working lives has curdled into doubt. 'I thought I'd get to retirement age and be on holiday every month,' said a 67-year-old from Cambridgeshire. 'Life's got more difficult and, you know, it is a little bit scary.'

They are more educated than other 'tribes', with 27 per cent holding higher qualifications with a relatively even split between low and medium education.

They are not extremists. Many still believe in fairness, community and compassion. But they feel the system has stopped working for 'people like us'. They volunteer at the library, tend the church fête, and feel personally affronted by boarded-up shops and shuttered youth centres. 'It's soul-destroying,' they say, and it is. They are not angry so much as heartbroken – believing their country could be kinder, cleaner, prouder, if only someone in power cared enough to try. 'It shouldn't be right in this day and age,' said a 60-year-old from Bristol, 'that people go to work but still have to go to food banks to feed their children.'

Immigration is a prism for wider questions of fairness. 'People are afraid of talking about immigration because they're scared of being called racist,' said a 60-year-old from Hertfordshire. 'But it's not about being racist. It's about looking after all the people in this country who are poor, starving. We can't keep supporting everybody.' Another added: 'If I ruled this country, I'd look after our own people first.'

For the Melancholy Middle, populism is not a crusade but a cry – for control, decency and recognition. They might nod along with Farage, but many stop short of devotion. They are anxious not irretrievable. If mainstream politics can restore hope and rebuild pride of place, the Melancholy Middle can still return to the mainstream.

5. *The Civic Pragmatists: not rebels but reformers*

Finally come the Civic Pragmatists. They too make up about one in five potential Reform voters, and are almost as gender-balanced as the Melancholy Middle. Politically they are the most foot-loose of all five tribes: 59 per cent say they intend to vote Reform, but 41 per cent are only considering it, and the data shows that this group considers voting for the broadest spread of potential parties, including Labour, Lib Dems and Greens.

They are noticeably younger than the other tribes: nearly half are under 50, though just over a quarter are over 65.

Financially, they look similar to the Melancholy Middle – 44 per cent are comfortable and only around one in seven are struggling. They might be a 30-something professional who rents a flat they can barely afford and works hard for a promotion that never comes. They don't hate the world but they're just tired of running up a down escalator. 'My focus has changed from thriving to making ends meet,' they admit, half embarrassed, half furious. They are not cynical. They are impatient.

'I feel like there's no end in sight,' said another, a 33-year-old from Bristol. 'Whenever your wages go up, all the bills go up ... we are constantly moving the goalposts further away.' They are more financially secure than other groups, more likely to feel in control of their daily lives, and less inclined to see their local area as in freefall. Educationally they are quite a mix: almost a quarter have a degree but 37 per cent have low qualifications.

Their adult lives have been lived under the long shadow of austerity. They want fairness, energy and, above all, competence. They don't care who delivers change so long as someone finally gets a grip. They value fairness, decency and hard work. They grumble about immigration but detest its weaponisation. They roll their eyes at Farage even as they concede he sometimes 'sounds like a real person'. One 26-year-old from Manchester summed it up: 'My share could be better if money was spent more wisely ... going after people who actively avoid paying their fair share.'

What they share with other Reform considerers is a frustration with politics-as-usual. '[Politicians] are completely out of touch with the normal general public,' said the woman from Bristol. 'Totally untrustworthy.' Yet they are not consumed by despair. 'It's going to be absolutely stinking for the younger generation,' said a 43-year-old from Edinburgh. 'They've been mis-sold a future by the powers that be.'

On paper, they look more like the progressive base than the populist hardcore. They are more worried about climate change, more supportive of universal services, more open to closer ties with Europe. They resent tax avoidance and waste, and bridle at governments that 'go after OAPs and farmers' while letting 'millionaires and rich landowners' off the hook. If they flirt with Reform, it is as a reluctant protest vote. 'I don't really admire him,' said the woman from Bristol, 'but if I had to choose the best of a bad bunch, I'd look into Nigel Farage … he's more in touch with a real-life person.'

Civic Pragmatists are pragmatic patriots: proud of their country, tired of its dysfunction. They do not want to burn the system down. They want it to work again. They are Reform's least committed supporters – and mainstream politics' greatest opportunity.

Shared wounds, different worlds

Painting a picture of these tribes together reveals why populists are winning and what it will take to beat them. But for all their unity in frustration, there are some deep divides between these tribes. While all five tribes share annoyance and pessimism, their values diverge dramatically. At one extreme, the Disgusted Disruptors and the Left-Behind Collectivists crave a strong leader who will 'break the rules' – an authoritarian instinct shared by around 70–80 per cent of each group. But at the other end, only 42 per cent of Civic Pragmatists agree.

On climate change, the gulf widens further: just 18–29 per cent of Disgusted Disruptors and Left-Behind Collectivists respectively see the necessity of action as urgent, compared to more than three-quarters of Civic Pragmatists. Support for universal welfare and the NHS also splits the coalition: the Left-Behind Collectivists and Civic Pragmatists show the strongest backing for social protection, while Digusted Disruptors are much cooler. Europe is another fault line. Only 14 per cent of Disgusted Disruptors want closer ties with the EU. Among Civic Pragmatists, nearly two-thirds do.

This tells us something vital: mainstream parties can split the populist coalition – not with a foolish attempt at mass conversion – but by taking selective aim at those groups who might actually change their mind, the groups we christen the Melancholy Middle and the Civic Pragmatists. But this mission of persuasion will not be easy. It will require some very difficult choices and a grip on issues that progressives often like to avoid. Across every single one of these tribes, immigration comes top of the list of issues they believe are facing Britain. Even among Civic Pragmatists and the Melancholy Middle – the most moderate groups – there is far greater agreement than the national average with the idea that 'immigration is a threat to British culture and values'. The cultural anxiety is real and so is the sense of loss.

But this mission of restoring fairness, reciprocity and order to immigration reform must be part of a much wider project. Populist voters might be divided on what leadership and progress looks like, but they share a deep sense that hard work no longer pays. Across the Reform electorate, the living-standards crisis is the root of disillusion.

Populist voters feel under financial pressure or frustrated with their progress in life. They live in precarious places. They are pessimistic about the future, convinced the odds are stacked against them. They feel dispossessed of the place they thought they had earned in the queue of life – hence their anger at an immigration system they see as unfair. And they are driven to distraction by broken politics that has failed to keep its promises. If centrist parties cannot offer progress on living standards, a restoration of pride in place, plausible optimism about the future, a fair immigration system and a state that is visibly back on voters' side, they will go on losing.

History teaches one blunt truth: you cannot beat a force you refuse to understand. Unless we trace the wellsprings of anger that nourish the populist project, we cannot craft a politics powerful enough to stop their surge. So we must begin by understanding the five deep roots of the populist appeal.

3

The End of Hope

A few weeks after President Trump's re-election, I found myself on the shores of Lake Geneva, strolling beside the Centre William Rappard, the home of the World Trade Organization. It is a place of vanishing ambition: a villa built for the League of Nations remade into a temple of post-Cold War optimism. With its polished floors, cool grey stone walls, warm woods, and spectacular narrative-realist murals celebrating 'work in abundance', 'benefits of leisure' and 'universal joy', it projects calm, order – and optimism. Where better to house the headquarters of a new institution to referee world trade, keep markets open and help globalise the economy, whereby – so the theory ran – we would all be better off.

But that morning, the serenity belied a rising panic among officials surveying an earthquake. That week President Trump had torn up the order they worked so hard to defend. Tariffs. Trade wars. A rule-book shredded. Yet the moment had been coming for years.

Country	Average annual wage rise, 2000-2008	Average annual wage rise, 2008-2023
Greece	2.20%	-1.88%
Italy	0.43%	-0.43%
Netherlands	0.73%	-0.34%
Spain	0.34%	-0.25%
United Kingdom	1.90%	0.29%
Austria	0.95%	0.30%
Belgium	0.36%	0.31%
France	1.03%	0.44%
Germany	0.26%	0.91%
Poland	1.61%	2.44%
Canada	1.41%	0.72%
United States	0.96%	1.06%
Czechia	4.21%	1.51%
Slovak Republic	3.14%	1.55%
Slovenia	2.76%	1.71%
Hungary	4.28%	1.88%
Average	1.66%	0.64%

The WTO opened its doors in 1995, just as Francis Fukuyama published his famous tract which declared that liberal democracy had reached a high-water mark that might be 'the end point of mankind's ideological evolution'.[1] Three decades later it did not feel like the end of history for millions of people. It felt like the end of hope. What began as a remarkable dream – 'a world without walls'[2] – has

Change	$ per week 2000-2008	$ per week 2008-2023
-4.1%	-US$14.82	-US$11.67
-0.9%	-US$4.51	-US$4.26
-1.1%	-US$5.01	-US$4.94
-0.6%	-US$2.59	-US$2.65
-1.6%	US$3.44	US$3.58
-0.6%	US$4.11	US$4.37
-0.0%	US$4.30	US$4.57
-0.6%	US$4.68	US$5.16
0.6%	US$10.58	US$12.12
0.8%	US$14.44	US$20.71
-0.7%	US$8.60	US$9.65
0.1%	US$14.28	US$16.89
-2.7%	US$8.95	US$11.15
-1.6%	US$8.27	US$10.77
-1.0%	US$15.61	US$20.32
-2.4%	US$10.16	US$12.67
38%	US$0.00	US$0.00

become a reality of struggle, insecurity and communities left behind. In the West's heartlands, the promise that every generation would do better than the last has collapsed. The escalator stopped. For millions it began to run in reverse. This is where populism begins: with the great disillusion. Unless we understand this rupture we simply cannot decode populism nor assemble a project to defeat it.

Under pressure

As we read in Chapter 1, the alpha of modern populism is what we might call the great disillusion. In the glades that opened when the Berlin Wall fell, we built a global economy of trade and technology that was at first an extraordinary boon. But over time, thanks to a cascade of bad decisions, that economy has handed extraordinary riches to a lucky few while leaving millions behind. The prize and price of trade and tech are hopelessly out of balance. And this should have been anticipated.

The father of free-trade theory, David Ricardo, said a lot about the gains of trade but almost nothing about who gained. What was heralded as a tide to lift all boats has in fact left fleets divided – some sailed on new currents, others were stranded on the shore. As Ben Page, former chief executive of Ipsos MORI, memorably put it, 'we created a society of haves, have-nots and have yachts'.

Then came the Great Financial Crisis. Sam Freedman calls it 'the moment when everything got worse'. Productivity collapsed. Wages flat-lined. Services hollowed out. The escalator of opportunity, already slowing, juddered. In Britain, austerity delivered the longest wage stagnation since the Napoleonic Wars. Councils went bust. Local services crumbled. Thousands of food banks had to be created to help feed families and children. In Europe, technocratic bailouts shredded democratic sovereignty. In the United States, the Tea Party erupted, attacking the betrayal of Main Street by Wall Street. By 2016, Donald Trump was railing against a 'rigged system'. The crisis didn't just trigger a downturn; the clear-up operation discredited elites and fractured trust. As Evelyne Hübscher and Thomas Sattler show,[3] every wave of austerity across Western Europe has been followed by a surge in populism. In the UK, it helped create the conditions for Brexit.[4]

For workers across the richer parts of the world, the post-2008 years were brutal. Average earnings in major OECD economies grew just 0.6 per cent a year – a 60 per cent collapse from the late-1990s trend.[5] To put that in perspective, consider this: if your pay is growing at 1.6 per cent a year, it takes a generation for your wages to double; about 44 years. But if your wages grow by 0.6 per cent a year, it takes an era for your wages to rise by the same extent; around 106 years to be precise.[6]

And averages mask the worst pain: low-income workers saw even weaker growth while housing costs rose three times faster than median incomes. By 2019, one in five middle-income households across the OECD was spending more than they earned. Then came the contagion of Covid and the conflict in Ukraine, spiking both government debt and prices. By 2023, real wages were still below pre-Covid levels in 20 OECD countries. The Tony Blair Institute captured the consequences: 'In the second half of the 20th century, living standards … doubled each generation. The observation that this has stalled – and the fear it will go into reverse – have fed the appetite for insurgent politics.'[7]

The stories behind these statistics now shape our politics. The ethnographic work in the Faster Horses study confirms that these big trends cratered the lives of ordinary voters.[8] Like so many I meet in my constituency, our research heard from people who have 'always worked, always paid their way', yet feel they are slipping backwards. Many left school young, entered steady jobs, raised families and played by the rules. But the rules, they believe, have changed. Wages lag behind prices. Bills rise faster than pay. Savings feel futile. As one man put it, you can work full-time and still end up broke by Friday. For many, even small pleasures feel out of reach. 'Getting a cup of coffee and a cheese toastie in Costa – that's a luxury I can't afford anymore,' one woman told researchers.

Around two-thirds of Reform's most ardent supporters say they are worse off than they expected to be at this stage of life, while approximately half expect their wealth to fall over the next decade. 'We've worked all our lives and have so little to show for it,' said one. 'I thought by now I'd be able to take my foot off the pedal and enjoy life a bit more,' said another. 'But there's never any luxuries. It looks like I'll be grinding away for ever.' Yet four in five believe 'people like me don't get our fair share' of public spending. This is not the anti-state libertarianism of elite populism. It is a cry for fairness from people who feel they kept their side of the bargain but government and employers broke theirs. Their politics does not begin with ideology. It begins with injustice.

These voters are not – on paper – Britain's poorest. Reform-considering voters have median incomes only slightly below the national figure,[9] and similar levels of wealth. But Reform-minded voters are far more likely to be disappointed with their progress in life – compared to their hopes and compared to their perception of others. In particular, our Disgusted Disruptors and Left-Behind Collectivists are far more likely to feel they have fared worse than others when it comes to thinking about whether they are as well off as they wanted to be at this stage of life. But the distress is more acute than that. They feel more deprived, more insecure and more pessimistic.

Several things might explain this.

Reform-minded voters on average left school earlier – and so may not have the same power in a competitive and fast-changing labour market. Constituencies with fewer graduates were far more likely to vote Reform; in fact, the share of adults with a degree was the single strongest predictor of low Reform support. TBI's Deltapoll found that 46 per cent of those considering Reform left school at 16 or younger; only 22 per cent pursued education beyond 21. And there was generally a reason for this: a twist of fate, a parent who died, a family that fractured, an urgent need to earn.

But there is a second force at work. Today's distress is particularly acute among Britain's 'mid-life swing generation' (aged 35–59), identified by Jane Green's research,[10] using a 16,000-person panel. This is the group juggling four sets of costs: mortgages or insecure housing, childcare bills, low savings and high unsecured debts. Almost half (41 per cent) report feeling economically insecure,[11] triggering what Green calls 'a considerable amount of psychological distress'.[12] They lack a safety net and worry deeply about retirement. These voters are not the destitute; they are the squeezed. And squeezed people vote. Among insecure voters aged 50–60, Reform UK has surged in support.[13]

By the time of the 2024 elections – when perhaps 2 billion people went to vote – the combination of stalling wages and soaring prices was a vote-killer for mainstream parties. In the US, Progressive Policy Institute polling showed inflation was the number-one issue for 46 per cent of working-class voters. Women were 'significantly more concerned' about the cost of living than about cultural flashpoints. As PPI's Will Marshall put it, Democrats 'got blindsided by inflation [which] ... working-class voters linked ... to high government spending'.[14]

Across Europe the pattern was similar. In France, food prices rose 20 per cent in two years; electricity, over 70 per cent in five years.[15] In the shops, even middle-class families were counting every euro. In Italy, working-class living standards are no better than they were at the turn of the century.[16] In Germany, PPI captured the confession of one former SPD voter in West Germany who said, 'I don't really like opening my bills anymore ... since everything became more expensive.'[17] Almost 100 per cent of AfD voters described the economic situation as poor.[18]

But the toll is not only financial. It is emotional. It eats at dignity and worth. One woman in Britain told researchers she had not been on holiday since 1998: 'I've got no meaningful life. I might as well be dead.'

Claire Ainsley captured the psychology for me: 'It's partly wealth, living standards, earning power, but it's as much dignity as anything else. And status.' Economic stagnation wounds both the wallet and the spirit, robbing people of respect, belonging and recognition. And, Claire reminded me, this pre-dates the crash of 2008: 'This didn't start with the financial crisis. It started when the centre-left began losing working-class voters – driven by an educational divide.' And it has a particular effect on the places people call home.

Precarious communities

We used to say in politics that 'all politics is local'. Now, it is hyper-local. The state of streets you walk, your estate, the little stretch between your front door, the green space where you walk the dog, and the shops where you buy the milk has a profound effect on how you feel about your life, how you think you're doing, and what future you see ahead.[19] For populist-minded voters, that everyday landscape of home feels like it is in free fall and nothing can stop it. Nostalgia has always fuelled the populist imagination, but I'm now convinced it is a nostalgia for a local way of life that feels long gone.

Today's cartography of discontent shows that the places left behind are the places most likely to vote for populists.[20] Across both the US and Europe, the atlas of populist revolt outlines a landscape of economic decline. Studies show 'grievances over an increasingly uneven distribution of resources ... especially between leading and left-behind regions, are good predictors of support for far-right populist parties'.[21]

Look at America. President Trump's support came roaring out of the hollowed-out heartlands: Appalachian coal country, rural Mississippi and the Rust Belt counties of the Midwest. In 2016, Trump's vote share was strongest where Chinese imports had gutted manufacturing – towns in Michigan, Wisconsin, Pennsylvania and North Carolina where factories shut, wages stagnated and futures collapsed. America's voters are spread across the nation in a checker-board of 3,100 counties. Back in 1996, Bill Clinton won nearly half of them. In 2024, Kamala Harris won just 427. Trump? He swept 2,633. Those places tend to have more teen mothers, worse health, lower school enrolment and a five-year shorter life expectancy than Democratic states. J. D. Vance's *Hillbilly Elegy* captured this world: talent may be everywhere, but wealth is not.

Sixty per cent of America's wealth is concentrated in just 382 of its counties, creating a new geography of class.[22]

In a brilliant post-election analysis, Bill Galston and Elaine Kamarck concluded, 'We have a new class-based politics reinforced by the fact that prosperity in twenty-first-century America is concentrated in metropolitan areas.'[23]

Poorer counties and rural-small-town-left-behind America voted Trump, as Professor Ben Ansell and David Adler spotted back in 2019.[24] On stage recently, Ben explained how to read this from house prices: 'Homeowners who lived in areas with stagnant or declining house prices are the Trump base.' By contrast, Clinton voters were 'the winners of rising residential wealth'. The *Financial Times*'s Joel Luss found the same pattern: cities with slower post-2020 income growth swung hardest to Trump.[25]

In France, Marine Le Pen's party has surged in low-skill, high-unemployment towns in the north and anxious Mediterranean suburbs. Macron swept Paris and the places that drink Nespressos; the Rassemblement National swept forgotten France.

In Germany, the AfD dominates the deindustrialised east. As one switcher put it: 'The typical worker used to be in industry, coal mining … now we're not producing anything anymore.' In Italy, Meloni's FdI is strongest in low-income, high-unemployment southern provinces.

An analysis of Britain reveals the same story. The Brexit base was not in the Home Counties but in left-behind industrial towns. Today, Reform polls strongest where manufacturing has gone, business activity is weak and rent growth lags.[26] When I looked at house prices in high

Reform-voting seats in 2024,[27] I found they were a third lower than the national average. That is almost £120,000 less.[28]

But statistics only take us so far. Our research shows *why* the precarity of place matters. Reform-considering voters are far more likely to say their local area has declined.[29] Almost two-thirds say so – rising to more than 80 per cent among the most committed Reform supporters[30] – crucially, these residents who are also far less likely to believe 'there is a good sense of community spirit in my area'. And their stories tell us why they feel this.

The sense of decline in local places is visceral amongst Reform supporters. High streets once full of pride are now symbols of decay. Once they were where we met; now they are what we mourn. For many, the triggers are not abstract forces like GDP or inflation but the visible signs of neglect: litter, graffiti, antisocial behaviour, boarded-up shops, shuttered libraries and youth centres, fly-tipping, potholes, and weeds growing through cracked pavements.[31]

'It's soul-destroying to see our area turn to crap,' said one respondent in Faster Horses' ethnographic study. What makes it worse is the feeling of abandonment – that neither politicians, nor councils, nor the police care anymore.

We found a vicious cycle. When Reform-minded voters talk about decline, two words recur: shops and crime. Crime drives people indoors; closed shops extinguish civic pride.

Communities experiencing higher crime rates vote for Reform in bigger numbers.[32] Poverty plays its part: 'Our local Range has started tagging washing powder – because grans are nicking it,' said one woman in the study.

Focus groups repeatedly highlight young people as both symptom and source of neighbourhood decline, blaming crime, drugs and antisocial behaviour on under-stimulated youth.[33] Yet everyone knows the cause is a collapse in youth services.

This lack of care triggers retreat. 'Nobody likes to go out on an evening no more,' a woman in West Bromwich told researchers ICON.[34] 'You don't feel safe.' Civic pride withers. Communities fracture. And pessimism about the future grows deeper.

Pessimism

Over time, persistent disappointment asphyxiates aspiration. Ben Page captured the scale of the shift for me: 'At the beginning of the century, only about 10–12 per cent of people expected their children to be poorer than them ... by 2019 that figure had gone to 45 per cent.' This is, as he rightly says, a 'massive psychological shift'. It would be astonishing if it did not have a political effect. Across Western democracies the clearest measure of disillusion is this: most people now believe their children will be worse off than they are. Across six of the world's richest nations, a majority of so-called 'Outsiders' – who have all but given up on mainstream politics – expect living standards to fall for the next generation.[35]

The grind has ground so long that family after family today experiences inter-generational *downward* social mobility. Peter Kellner, the founder of YouGov, told me, 'A large part of the rise of populism can be traced to younger generations who fear they will never do as well as their parents.' Professor Jane Green has a sharper phrase: millions no longer feel they are 'have-nots' – they are 'won't-haves'. Sustained financial pressure coupled with life in precarious communities has one inevitable result: pessimism.

Arlie Hochschild found something similar among Tea Party voters in Louisiana: people who felt they had been 'waiting in line for ever' for the American Dream, only to watch the queue move backwards. If you were born before 1950, your income rose with age; after 1950, it did not. Economist Phillip Longman calls it 'lifetime downward mobility' – and populist supporters feel it most acutely.[36]

In Britain, this despair is now endemic. Among Reform-minded voters, only 18 per cent believe today's young people will have a better life than their parents. Just 26 per cent expect their own wealth to rise over the next decade; 38 per cent expect it to fall – ten points higher than the national average.[37]

And the gloom is not limited to personal finances. Eighty-eight per cent believe the UK itself has declined. Many feel the situation is beyond broken. 'I ask myself, can this country sustain itself in its present form? The answer is no,' said one focus-group participant. 'The future's not looking great.'

'It's just looking bleaker and bleaker for the country,' another person said. One said simply, 'I don't think my life is going to get any better. I feel like it's probably going to get worse.'

While the wider public tends to blame overstretched services, Reform-considerers speak instead of cultural erosion, crime and immigration. This is not mild dissatisfaction, and it has crystallised a clear view about the solution required: three-quarters of Reform-considerers we polled are willing to elect a 'strong leader' who is prepared to break the rules.

It is not hard to find voters with the same sentiment in Europe. 'We're all burnt out,' said one former SPD voter from East Germany who now backs the AfD. 'The situation is going further downhill because of politics. It's very difficult for a normal person of my age to find a good job.'[38] In Germany – so long a byword for economic strength – 57 per cent of AfD voters now believe today's children will be poorer than their parents.[39]

Dispossession

In my East Birmingham constituency, many of the residents I serve – under acute pressure, trapped in precarious communities, pessimistic about the future, seized with a sense that life had simply not proven fair – are angry about immigration. That is, immigration regardless of background or ethnicity. In our research, it is the single most important issue uniting Reform-minded voters, cutting across economic fear, cultural anxiety and moral resentment, supplying a 'perfect storm' of anger. In our polling amongst Reform-minded voters, the data is clear: 88 per cent believe immigration threatens British culture and values; 79 per cent think it has been mostly bad for the country; just 3 per cent say it has been mostly good.

Immigration has become the lightning rod for a wider collapse in confidence, not only in whether politics works, but in whether politics can be fair. We found Reform-minded voters feel they have faced hard knocks without help. As such, the perception of newcomers receiving help or assistance without making a contribution is not just frustrating – it is enraging, not least because the majority of the most zealous Reform voters see the world in zero-sum terms. In our polls, 51 per cent of Disgusted Disruptors agreed that 'there is only so much prosperity to go around – when some gain, others inevitably lose'. That is almost 20 points above the national average.

They therefore expect grit from others and feel fury at anything that looks like something for nothing. It breaks the ethic of reciprocity on which they have built their own survival. As one voter put it: 'Why should these people expect a free ride when I've had to work for everything?'

Of course, there are extremists. But, on the whole, what I hear is not xenophobia but hurt. In the moral economy of most Reform voters, the rule is simple: you put in, then you get out. Many feel today's system breaks that rule – rewarding those who have not contributed while those who worked hard pay the bill. Worse, many feel they cannot speak honestly about it: 'People are afraid of talking about it because they're scared of being called racist,' one woman told us. 'It's not about race. It's about looking after people here who are poor, starving.'

The feelings we hear in Britain rhyme with the 'deep story' Arlie Hochschild found in Louisiana: people in a long line under the hot sun, waiting for the American Dream, only to find the line moving backwards. They believe newcomers are cutting ahead – accelerating the 'cultural backlash' amongst the older majority described by Pippa Norris and Ronald Inglehart, who feel their way of life is ignored by policymakers and mocked in the media.

In 2024, the Democrats' record on immigration became a force multiplier for these sentiments. As Bill Galston and

Elaine Kamarck argued, 'Democrats need to understand just how badly the Biden administration's mishandling of immigration hurt Kamala Harris's chances.'[40] Between 2020 and 2023, border crossings surged past 7 million. Biden had denounced Trump's cruelty – but struggled to offer control. Progressive groups opposed tougher enforcement. But voters were furious. 'The situation is just a dumpster fire,' said one Pennsylvania swing voter.[41] 'My son can't find an apartment,' said another, 'but everybody comes pouring in from foreign countries and suddenly makes an apartment right away.'[42]

That sense of unfairness is populism's accelerant – and not just for white voters. Michael Tesler finds that, between 2020 and 2024, the number of Hispanic and Black voters who believed 'immigrants drain national resources' rose sharply.[43] In PPI's survey, working-class Hispanics narrowly preferred Trump to Harris on immigration. President Trump's 'they/them' ad targeting Harris – mocking Harris for cultural liberalism – became the most-cited reason not to vote for her in swing states and drew on deep-set cultural anxieties and economic fears fused into the populists' core story: the nation is full, the government is failing and the elites don't care.

Across Europe the pattern repeats. Radical-right parties have fused populism with nativism into welfare chauvinism: the idea that public services and protections belong to the native-born. In Provence-Alpes-Côte d'Azur, Félicien Faury found residents railing not simply at 'Arabs' or 'Turks' but at nursery queues, broken schools, shuttered high streets and benefits they believe are diverted to 'layabouts' who 'don't deserve it'.[44] In Germany – which ranked immigration concerns higher than anywhere else surveyed by the Tony Blair Institute – voters rewarded the party they felt 'spoke out early': the AfD. 'The main parties only speak about immigration during the election,' said one former SPD voter. 'The AfD has spoken out for a long time.'[45]

Yet take a step back and we can see a broader story still. Work from British Future shows that most Britons occupy what they call the 'Balancer Middle': those who want migration controlled, not closed; managed fairly, not cynically.[46] Nearly half accept that immigration supports growth, and large majorities back resettlement for refugees from Ukraine or Hong Kong. Yet successive governments, chasing headlines not results, have let the debate be defined by numbers rather than by competence. The public's real frustration lies less with migrants than with the absence of order. And that is part of a wider force driving voters towards populist parties; the profound sense that government is broken.

Broken politics

In the circumstances, you may not be surprised to learn that voters who feel their lives are buckled, their dreams betrayed, their communities spiralling out of their control in an economy where the rules are rigged against them – while others cut ahead in the queue – are furious with those they see as the authors of their agony: the politicians they elect to serve them. Democracy once loved for its promise is now distrusted for its performance.

When Peter Kellner kicked off our seminar series on populism at St Antony's College, Oxford, he began with a clarifying truth: 'that democracy has always been both a moral and an instrumental project'.[47] We value it. But it has to work. 'In the main,' explained Peter, 'populist voters are NOT ideological ... What they DO want ... is honest, competent government that raises living standards, keeps our streets safe and provides decent schools and hospitals.' Right now, they do not believe they get it – and do not see much of a choice between traditional mainstream parties.

For decades, globalisation's rules narrowed political choices. Before the 2008 American election Alan Greenspan was asked who he preferred for President. '[I]t hardly makes any difference,' he replied, 'the world is governed by market forces.'[48] Capital mobility, trade commitments and bond-market pressure pushed left and right towards the same narrow centre. The financial crash, geopolitical shocks and Covid only tightened the parameters. As debts soared and interest rates rose, so choices narrowed.[49] *The Economist* labelled it the 'deficit–populism doom loop':[50] when politicians appease markets, voters revolt; when they appease voters, markets revolt. To many people, it simply feels like the system is not just broken – but rigged.

Kelly Beaver, chief executive of Ipsos MORI, put it plainly: '[A] majority of people ... believe ... the state is rigged for the rich and powerful. The elites are not working for people like me.'[51] Our polling confirms this. The most zealous Reform voters are far more likely to believe 'life in Britain is a lottery – you have to be born in the right family to succeed', or that 'the economy is rigged to advantage the rich and powerful', and far less likely to believe 'a hard day's work delivers a fair day's pay'.

Across the developed world, Kelly told me, people increasingly believe 'the state is not providing for the future and not helping solve their problems'. Voters today are more likely 'to believe that the state is broken than the state is working in their favour', Kelly went on. That, she added, is 'an optimal environment for populist sentiment to thrive'.

Our British polling bears this out. Well over half of hardcore Reform voters say they are 'disgusted', 'angry' or 'frustrated' with the way politics works – and 80 per cent say traditional parties do not care about people like them. The ethnographic work we studied showed not passive disillusionment but active, seething distrust. Politicians are seen as out of touch, incompetent and in league with elites who care nothing for ordinary people. As campaign group 38 Degrees put it, Reform voters 'are frustrated, angry, fearful. They feel unheard' and profoundly believe the political system is broken. As one voter put it: 'I don't feel connected to them. I feel frustrated. They're out of touch with the real struggles that people like me face – juggling bills, working all the time, worrying how the bills are going to be paid. They just don't understand.'

America reached the same conclusion in 2024. Seventy-four per cent of voters told exit polls they were angry or dissatisfied with the direction of the country. Just 6 per cent said they were optimistic. 'The last four years have been so hard,' one told a PPI focus group. Again and again, the word voters used was 'broken'.[52]

Europe echoes this. Satisfaction with democracy has plummeted across the continent.[53] In Germany, the drop is sharpest among voters without degrees.[54] 'There's a gap between politics and us,' one German voter said.

'And the gap is widening.'[55] In France, Italy and the Netherlands, the working class increasingly feel politics has become a closed shop – run by a distant elite, answering to itself.

Among Reform voters in Britain, the anger often centres on bad choices. Taxes too high. Spending unfair. Money wasted. Most Reform-considering voters believe taxes are too high, that government money is wasted on the wrong things and that they do not get their fair share of public spending. Among Disgusted Disruptors, more than 80 per cent told us taxes are excessive, and the same proportion agreed that 'people like me do not get our fair share' – Reform voters are almost twice as likely as the average UK voter to feel this way. It is a combustible mix: economic squeeze, dashed expectations and the sense that others are rewarded at their expense. In America, Democrats made similar mistakes. One strategist told me: 'Every time Democrats talk more about identities than economics, Trump gains ground.'

Tim Ryan, the former Democratic Congressman from Ohio, was blunt: 'We lost the emotional connection to the working class. Cycle after cycle … we looked out of touch.' Trump, by contrast, 'talked about jobs, the price of eggs, and the people who waited years to get here while others walked across the border'.

Peter Hyman, who studied the 2024 US presidential race up close, told me Democrats now represent 'a coalition of comfort': the winners of the tech, finance and property booms – and have grown detached from those left behind. Worse, progressives responded to discontent with what Peter called the 'seven deadly sins': patronisation, complacency, abstraction, censoriousness, gullibility, conservativeness (defending broken institutions) and blandness.

The result, as Ben Page warns, is a hunger for easy answers. 'Social democracy hasn't delivered ... so people say: give me simple promises. That sounds good.' Kelly Beaver saw the same dynamic across the 2024 elections: the public were willing 'to roll the dice' on well-known disruptors – Farage, Le Pen, Wilders – because the mainstream no longer felt worth the risk.

And so, a stark conclusion emerges: voters who feel abandoned, exploited, unheard and over-taxed reach for the same remedy – a strong leader willing to break the rules. In Britain, 75 per cent of potential Reform voters agree, compared to 47 per cent of voters nationally. As one Trump supporter told Peter Hyman at a rally: 'We know he's an arsehole ... but we want a disruptor.'

Trump was less admired, rather hired – to smash the system. To punish the people and institutions voters feel have punished them. His appeal was visceral. He wasn't a reformer so much as an instrument of revenge. Dame Deborah Mattinson, who has spent months listening to American voters with PPI, once asked a focus group what kind of drink or car captured each candidate. For President Trump, the answer came back instantly: 'Dump truck ... owning the road, not to be argued with.' 'He's like neat whisky,' said another, 'he gives it to you straight.' Kamala Harris, by contrast, was described as 'a watered-down cocktail' or compared to 'a flimsy Kia'.

These are the wellsprings of populism today. They are deep. They are powerful. But simply understanding the demands of voters does not explain why populists are winning. Anger alone does not change politics. To truly understand why populists are winning we must listen to what populist leaders *supply*: the arguments they make, the words they use, the campaigns they run. For what populists have learned better than anyone is how, like political alchemists, to turn anger into power.

4

What's the Message?

When the British prime minister Sir Keir Starmer paid his first visit to President Trump in the Oval Office, he carried with him an invitation from the King. Amongst the media pack on hand to record the moment for posterity was the BBC's Political Editor, Chris Mason, who knew that somehow he needed to put himself in the President's line of sight if he was to land an early question. Thinking on his feet, he shouted out, 'What does the letter say, Mr President?' And so, on live television, the President opened his message from the Palace to read out what he called 'a lovely letter' inviting him to Britain for a second state visit.

As the afternoon wore on and the President serenely took question after question, Chris realised something important about the President's communication style. As he put it to me over lunch one day, 'This was statecraft as stagecraft.' He is right. But what is the populists' winning script?

Around the world, populists are re-inventing the way we argue, appeal and advance a political cause. By some estimates,[1] the volume of populist rhetoric across 40 major countries has doubled in the last 20 years. I am not surprised. Today's populists are amongst the best communicators in the world; better than mainstream politicians and better masters of new digital channels. Why? Because good communication requires one thing above all: clarity about what we are trying to say. For too long, mainstream politics has offered word salads while populists holler a *cri de coeur*. They offer simple stories for complex times. By contrast today's mainstream politicians too often fail to convey the necessities of all political communication: their motives, their purpose and their strength to ride the tides of fortune in this unpredictable world and make sure everything will turn out fine. Without these essentials it is impossible to build a brand that cuts through the digital smog that suffocates modern life. But through this smog, populists offer clarity.

As we saw in chapter one, defining populism is not easy but, in its broadest terms, populism rests on a claim to speak for the people and a denunciation of elites. Authoritarian populists, however, are much sharper. Their communication helps them win because it offers a conversational but arresting style and a clear sense of direction that, it turns out, rests on a consistent set of three core messages. This, like dark magic, is powerful because it taps the deeps of our human nature and is married to centuries of political philosophy. It is a hell of a project.

Let us start with style, where we find populists offer a beguiling blend of hard and soft. On the one hand there is the steel. Look no further than three of the most baleful examples from slogan land: Make America Great Again; Take Back Control; Get Brexit Done. Each acts as a sort of 'Evil Parrot.'[2] They frame people's desires (and prejudices) and repeat them back like negative reinforcement freighted with frustration. You could preface each of these slogans with the phrase: 'I wish we could just …' They offer imperatives. They do not present a shop window of nice things to choose from. They present a singular, specific action. They are active. In particular, President Trump often uses what is known in linguistics as 'directive speech acts', where the speaker actually commands the listener to do something, like 'Look at Paris …' He addresses us directly as if continuing a conversation, creating immediacy and intimacy. Even his most recent election message – 'Kamala is for they/them. Trump is for you' – which lacked an imperative verb, delivered a rhetorical sense of command: 'choose Trump – reject Kamala.'

Populists have a habit of using naked, unashamedly self-interested, acquisitive hard verbs – 'get', 'take' or 'keep'.[3] They share a notion that we must all seize or hold on to something for ourselves – generally power or resources – because by implication it has been stolen from us – perhaps by a faceless elite or a newcomer to the country.

The subtlety is that populists wrap these hard edges in a conversational tone. They sound like friends while speaking like generals. To decode this, I worked with a talented young Oxford University researcher, Rick Foster, to build a clean database of scores of keynotes speeches made by right-wing populist leaders across the United Kingdom, North America, and Europe between 2010 and 2025. The selection includes campaign speeches, formal addresses and speeches to parliaments and Congress by the most prominent populist party leaders, including Donald Trump, Nigel Farage, Marine Le Pen, Giorgia Meloni and

Viktor Orbán. We ran their speeches through two complementary computational techniques to find both the patterns of words that co-occur most often together and, second, clusters of themes.[4]

The analysis helps reveal the way populist leaders speak in informal, colloquial, personal, conversational ways as if one were talking with friends rather than pitching to voters. Markers of the style show up in clustered contractions such as 'you're', 'we're', 'I've', 'that's', 'gonna', 'can't', 'won't', 'wouldn't', and 'couldn't', which are less common in formal political speeches. The frequent use of first and second-person pronouns ('I', 'we', 'you') enriches the conversational flavour, alongside colloquial language like 'folks', 'you know', 'let me tell you'.

Let us take one illustration of a recent attack on Sir Keir Starmer by the Reform UK politician Richard Tice:[5] 'don't worry Starmer's coming,' he declared, 'I'll start again, I much prefer the other name … Starmageddon … he's not got a clue how to grow the economy. Not a Scooby-Doo …' It is certainly not a formal style. Rather, it is classic populist lingo combining a derisive epithet (like Trump's 'Crooked Hillary'), colloquial allusion, comic diminishment and in-group signalling. It's an attempt to foster the sense that the speaker is 'one of us', someone who speaks openly and candidly as the appealing, authentic candidate in contrast to the establishment 'well-polished' politicians who have presided over the broken system that has so angered the populist voters.

But if that is the style, what is the substance? And why does it all work so well? As poets and anthropologists have long understood, human beings combine both the need for love and society and a yen for autonomy and agency. 'Man is broad,' declared Dostoevsky's tragic hero Dmitri in *The Brothers Karamazov*, 'too broad'.[6] We contain multitudes and contradictions. But multitudes must make decisions and politics is, in essence, the way social animals make collective choices around the five dilemmas that have defined our social life since the dawn of civilisation: us or them; freedom or fairness; old ways or new; conflict or consensus; fear or hope. In the centre-ground of politics we make nuanced trade-offs between these choices. Populists do not. They refuse trade-offs. Populists have a clear playbook: us not them; freedom not social justice; old not new; conflict not consensus; and, of course, fear not hope.

The way populists explain these choices is to play their politics like country music – three chords and the truth. The truth may be a mere 'kernel', as Lord Mandelson once said about President Trump,[7] but it turns out the chords rarely change. The first is patriotism and renewal. The second is the summons to struggle. The third is a nostalgic conservatism, a hunger for what has been lost.

It is a beguiling harmony: a glorification of the nation, an urgent call for sweeping change, and a yearning to take back control of what is slipping away. Three chords: pride, peril and the promise of return. Different tunes, same refrain. And here lies the paradox. The language of renewal is drenched in decline. The call to arms is wrapped in grievance. The dream of a future is shackled to the myths of the past. Populists promise movement, yet bind us to memory. They preach freedom, yet thrive on fear. They summon unity, yet prosper on division.

But the power of these themes today is that each taps into some deep psychology and some tried and tested, if contested, political philosophy.

Patriotism and renewal

No one will be surprised that the cornerstone of populist rhetoric is patriotism and renewal. It is the master key. Again and again, populist speeches return to a simple motif: the celebration of nation and national identity, spiced with the language of collective action and rebirth – and set, like a canvas by Caravaggio, against a tenebristic contrast of decline and decay.

When we look at the co-occurrence of words in this pattern, we see incantations of the country's name or people lit up far more frequently than in the text of a mainstream politician. In populist speeches, proper nouns and adjectives – like 'Britain', 'France', 'British', 'French', 'Americans' – sit together with positive descriptors like 'great' and 'good', collective action words like 'work' and 'together' and frequent references to 'time' and 'new' evoking a sense of national renewal, or making the country great again.

An illustrative quote from President Trump makes the point: 'A new chapter of American Greatness is now beginning,' he told the Joint Session of Congress in 2017. 'A new national pride is sweeping across our Nation. And a new surge of optimism is placing impossible dreams firmly within our grasp. What we are witnessing today is the Renewal of the American Spirit.'[8]

The language is so infectious in populist networks that, some distance from the White House, the newly elected Reform UK Mayor of Greater Lincolnshire could be heard aspiring to match the President's lofty vision. On her election night, Andrea Jenkyns declared nothing less than 'a new dawn in British politics, the rebuilding begins here ... The fightback to save the heart and soul of our great country has now begun ... Inch by inch, Reform will reset Britain to its glorious past.'[9]

This first direction in populist rhetoric creates the appeal to 'us', a mythical united national community of souls, 'we, the people'. By association, the speaker is patriot-in-chief, the strong leader driving the effort to work together in a national struggle on a brave and difficult journey back to the promised land, to greatness or its restoration. Populists talk about the nation in reverential terms, celebrate patriotism and proclaim the populist movement as the force by which greatness is protected or restored.

We know why this works. A patriotic defensive heroism has been a cornerstone of national stories since Gilgamesh fought monsters to protect Uruk. Patriotism may be, as Samuel Johnson put it, the 'last refuge of a scoundrel' but for politicians it is the oldest tune in the book. It is never a struggle for the sake of it but a sacrifice for the common good. It works because we are hard-wired to respond, as the appeal triggers the instincts that allowed us to survive thousands of years ago.

In our earliest days, prehistoric warfare was both frequent and lethal,[10] and so bands of humans, however jealous of their personal autonomy, learned to cooperate to survive. This instinct is now thought to be the evolutionary root of altruism, because the humans who came together best, survived best, and so this instinct distinguished the winners, whose genes survived, diffused and multiplied down the generations. Charles Darwin was amongst the first to note it.[11] In *The Descent of Man*, Darwin wrote: 'There can be no doubt that a tribe including many members who, from possessing in a high degree the spirit of patriotism, fidelity, obedience, courage, and sympathy, were always ready to aid one another, and to sacrifice themselves for the common good, would be victorious over most other tribes.' When it comes to humans, it is not the fittest that survive but the most cooperative.[12] Or, as the father of modern sociobiology Edward Wilson wrote, together with an American evolutionary biologist David Sloan Wilson, the best way to understand Darwin is simple: while 'selfishness beats altruism within groups ... altruistic groups beat selfish groups. Everything else is commentary.'[13] In modern times, this instinct is the root of patriotism, what writer Yuval Noah Harari calls the kind of 'imagined order'[14] that enables 'mass cooperation' well beyond the 150 people or so with whom we are able to conduct direct relationships. Our instinct to put aside our differences and combine with our neighbours to defend the common home is quite simply what has kept us alive for millennia. It is triggered most easily by the conjuring of a threat, which is why populists' speeches so often use the chiaroscuro technique of contrasting the light of patriotism with the darkness of decline.

A few speech extracts make the point. Take President Trump, who declared in 2015, 'Our country is in serious trouble. We don't have victories anymore. We used to have victories, but we don't have them.'[15] Nigel Farage supplies plenty of British parallels. Speaking when he launched his party manifesto in 2024, he declared: 'I genuinely feel that Britain is broken, that nothing actually works anymore, I feel increasingly we're broken socially.'[16] He made the same point when he announced he was standing for election: 'we're in social decline, and we're actually in a form of moral decline: we have forgotten who we are as a country.'[17]

WHAT'S THE MESSAGE?

It is a favourite argument of Viktor Orbán. Speaking to his party conference in the same year, he said: 'Before our eyes, the strong, peaceful, free and happy Europe that we love so much, and which we longed for all our lives under communism, *is in decline and is fracturing*'[18] (my italics).

This line of argument reaffirms the worldview of populist voters. But it also draws on a century of right-wing thinking. Like populist voters, populist thinkers are darkly pessimistic about the future, obsessed with decline, and their origin story can be traced back to the German historian Oswald Spengler, whose magnum opus, *The Decline of the West*,[19] was a bestseller in the 'morbid age' of the 1920s.

Spengler brought a huge innovation to the study of history. Like the English historian Arnold Toynbee who followed him, Spengler was convinced that the proper unit of historical study was a civilisation, not the nation, and that like all living organisms – humans, animals, flowers – every civilisation passes through the 'age-phases of the individual man' from the vigour of youth to the infirmity of old age. The West had then arrived in 'the early winter of full civilisation'.[20]

This decline-cult of Spengler's successors has now produced a small library of apocalyptic books with similar names, like *The Death of the West* (Pat Buchanan, 2001), *Germany is Abolishing Itself* (Thilo Sarrazin, 2010), *Suicide of France* (Eric Zemmour, 2014), *The Strange Death of Europe* (Douglas Murray, 2017), and *Le Suicide Occidental* (Jean-François Colosimo, 2020). You get the idea. They follow Spengler in two ways:[21] they share a focus on civilisational culture and a dark sense of the apocalyptic.

In this 'dark specialism', the French were early movers. Alain de Benoist, a key thinker in the French Nouvelle

Droit of the late 1960s, believed (like the French New Left) that political revolutions begin with intellectual revolutions.[22] Drawing on Spengler, de Benoist advanced the idea that an ethno-cultural homogeneity is essential for political and social order.

It is an idea that the far-right French writer Renaud Camus reprised in the following way: 'what makes countries, continents, cultures and civilisations what they are ... are the people and elites who have fashioned them and continued to embody them and their man-made essence.'[23] Nations, so the argument goes, are ethnically and culturally specific, organic, ancestral, not a civic or pluralistic concept. In the 1960s, De Benoist was anxious about the threat of the United States and Soviet Union, but his successors retrained their sights on immigration in general and Islam in particular. Whereas fascist writers were once obsessed with eugenics, today's populist doom-mongers obsess over demography and the cultural change they declare will follow if the locals have less kids and newcomers arrive, especially if the newcomers are either Muslim or Mexican.[24]

In a shelf of bestsellers ranging from the overtly racist to the plainly deranged, French authors sketched the same dark storyline. Jean Raspail's *The Camp of the Saints*,[25] Renaud Camus' polemic *Le Grand Remplacement*,[26] Eric Zemmour's *Suicide of France* and Michel Houellebecq's lurid tale of a Muslim Brotherhood French President,[27] all conjured apocalyptic visions of national collapse. The hard-right writers argue that progress, like allowing women to go to work,[28] universal college education, legalisation of homosexuality, contraception and abortion had together triggered a decline in the European birth rate and now newcomers to Europe were destined to replace the local population as they arrived in what Camus insists on labelling 'an invasion, a migratory tsunami' akin to 'reverse colonisation'.

Writers like Raspail and Houellebecq were said to have profoundly influenced the French far-right leader Marine Le Pen,[29] and together this sinister catalogue has seeded what has become known as identitarianism – a movement born in France in the early 2000s but which has spread across Europe. At its heart lies a dark conviction: that nations must wall themselves off, preserving a narrow vision of Christian, Greco-Roman and European heritage against the so-called 'threat' of immigration. Not a policy challenge, they insist, but an existential crisis. It is a movement that does not simply chase votes. It wages a culture war that seeks to defeat the liberal tradition and bend the common sense of a continent with slick branding, youth-focused campaigns and provocative stunts like Génération Identitaire. Its aim is simple but sinister: to launder exclusionary ideas until they look like cultural preservation, to repackage division as tradition, to turn fear into identity.

Bestselling British writers by contrast are a little milder,[30] generally avoiding identitarian prescriptions, but have in recent years become ever more extreme. In different ways,[31] the American Christopher Caldwell, Douglas Murray and Matt Godwin have all centred their work on the growth of immigration to Europe and the challenges of integration in Muslim communities.

Christopher Caldwell,[32] for example, argues that Muslim immigration threatens European culture, its tradition of tolerance and social safety nets. 'Islam', he argues, 'has broken a good many of the European customs, received ideas and state structures with which it has come into contact' because immigrants 'may not necessarily want a European life. They may want a third world life at a European standard of living.'[33]

'Europe', he argues, now 'finds itself in a contest with Islam for the allegiance of its newcomers. For now Islam is the stronger party in that contest'[34] and 'its spread will cumulatively spell a permanent and undesirable cultural alteration of their continent'.[35]

Douglas Murray takes the alarmism up a notch with a tour of European immigration and integration policy to conclude: 'The world is coming into Europe at precisely the moment that Europe has lost sight of what it is.'[36] The result? '[I]t is likely that our European culture ... will not survive.'[37]

But neither the French or the Brits have proved as influential as Pat Buchanan. A Catholic son of Washington, advisor to presidents and a three-time presidential candidate, Buchanan was the single most effective polemicist opposing the neo-conservatism of President George Bush. He proposed a paleoconservatism that championed the idea of a new nationalism,[38] and an American nation structured around a white, European heritage.[39] With his book *The Death of the West*, Buchanan translated Camus' *Great Replacement* into an American key, exporting Europe's paranoia into America's culture war. Taking aim at the 'the rise of a world socialist superstate',[40] the 'dechristianisation of America', combined together with modern life's 'freedom from family responsibilities', 'the menace of multiculturalism', Marxists and Mexicans (denounced as 'another race'),[41] Buchanan's thesis was wearyingly familiar: 'Kill a nation's faith,' he wrote, 'and its people will cease to reproduce. Foreign armies or immigrants then enter and fill the empty spaces.'[42]

WHAT'S THE MESSAGE?

Step back and the pattern is clear. Douglas Murray declares: 'Europe is committing suicide.'[43] Houellebecq announces: 'Europe had already committed suicide.' Camus says we are in for 'civil war'.[44] Zemmour insists 'we no longer have the same people, on the same land, speaking the same language, and obeying the same laws' and Pat Buchanan screams, 'The death of the west is not a prediction of what is going to happen, it is a depiction of what is happening now.'[45] Different voices, different words – but the same dirge: a West doomed, a civilisation in collapse. And it has profoundly shaped populist rhetoric.

We need merely survey a few of the populists' speeches to see the influence of these arguments. The literature of loss has become the language of campaigns. The Dutch politician Geert Wilders was an early mover. Back in 2009, he declared: 'Now, radical Muslims want to implement Sharia law into our Western societies. And they are very successful in doing so, helped by the Western cultural relativists.'[46] Viktor Orban uses similar language.[47] He told his party conference in 2015: 'We see that we have been invaded. Europe is under invasion, it looks like a battlefield, and what we have seen so far is just the tip of the iceberg.' Marine Le Pen is equally fond of the theme. In her conference speech of 2018 she railed against 'Cultural insecurity with the submersion of our countries by large, totally uncontrolled migrations of populations', which she argued was creating 'lawless areas among us, with the importation of morals or rules contrary to our values and in particular to our principles of secularism or respect for the freedom and integrity of women'.[48] Mr Farage, by contrast, tends to put a twist on the idiom by keeping the focus on crime. He told his party conference in 2024:

'I thought about what was happening on our streets – the rise of knife crime, the rise of gun crime, the fear of people even in the smartest parts of London to go out for a drink ... I thought about what mass uncontrolled immigration on a scale the likes of which we've never seen had done to divide our communities.'[49]

It is easy to see why populists lean on this tactic. As Jonathan Haidt shows, we are not creatures of reason alone but of instinct – instincts older than democracy itself. Some are the 'individualising virtues': care, fairness, liberty. Others are the 'binding virtues': loyalty, authority, sanctity. And when people feel under threat, those binding virtues can harden into authoritarian reflexes. And here is the danger. The virtues that bind us can also blind us. The instincts that once kept us safe can be turned into snares. And as Ezra Klein once observed, 'The simplest way to activate someone's identity is to threaten it, to tell them they don't deserve what they have, to make them consider that it might be taken away.' This is why populists revel in division.[50] It is a tried and trusted method. First, rouse fear. Foster a sense of threat. That makes it easier to call the people to arms and to cast yourself as the only shield against decline.

The struggle

The second pattern of words that emerged clearly in our analysis of populist rhetoric mashes together words that refer to the political processes of change, like 'election', 'vote', 'party', 'government', 'administration', 'change' and (in the UK) specific watershed terms such as 'Brexit'. In this word-pattern there is some reference to Europe (in the European speeches), implying a redefining of the nation's relationship with the EU, and the idea of 'newness' is a prominent feature; 'new' is frequently mentioned along with words such as 'government' or 'administration' to imply an upending of the status quo.

In this pattern of co-occurring words, we also see words like 'job' and 'work', which show up suggesting a promise to rebuild or change systems that are failing people (e.g. 'get the job done' rhetoric, or creating jobs for citizens). This is forward-looking, full of the promise of something better. It is an attempt to mobilise people to 'vote' for 'change' or something 'new'. It offers the contrast to the status quo – the 'administration' and 'government' – implying that they are ineffective or worse, and that change is required.

A study of topic-clustering adds to this picture. It shows the buttress to this content is a common rhetorical feature centred on the use of action- and combat-oriented language. Some of this is constructive. Fragments of this cluster include constructive action-oriented words like 'build' or 'lead'. Not all of this language is combative and destructive. But this cluster of words includes terms that imply action, struggle, and violent movement, like 'fight', 'win', 'battle', 'attack', 'defeat', 'struggle', 'push', 'change', 'lead', 'build' and 'save'.

These words collectively frame politics as a high-stakes conflict, as populists seek to mobilise maximum support and ensure a higher turnout of their supporters by energising them with fear and conflict, not hope or consensus. It is not a novel strategy. 'You have enemies?' said Winston Churchill. 'Good. That means you've stood up for something, sometime in your life.' When Ronald Reagan blazed onto the scene, the enemy was big government.[51] Populists now offer new antagonists; generally something foreign. But the tactic works because it conjures up the fear of loss, and as behavioural economics has confirmed, this fear of loss is far more powerful than hope.

The pioneers of behavioural economics, Daniel Kahneman and Richard Thaler, help us understand why. In their work, they explain that when making decisions, people attach values to gains and losses but these values tend to differ from real world probabilities of what might actually happen. A loss of something we already hold feels much worse than the joy that a new gain might bring. After a range of experiments, the Kahneman concluded that 'Roughly speaking, losses hurt about twice as much as gains make you feel good.' As a result we are driven more strongly to avoid losses than to achieve gains. Populists instinctively understand the politics of 'loss aversion'.

Together these themes are potent: a glorification of the nation that must be saved from a civilisational threat from 'others' in a great epic struggle to hold onto something you treasure but which is imperilled. But to this we must add one final chord in the populist hymn-book: a nostalgic restoration conservatism and a hunger to return to something lost. As a general rule, populists prefer old ways to new, especially if those old ways are 'lost'. They will always opt for the traditional over the novel regardless of whether the past has failed, because through the sepia tint of nostalgia anyone can make the past look nice. This is their winning message: a nation to love, an enemy to fear, a past to restore. And here, at least for now, populists have managed to straddle a division in Conservative thought that, in due course, may prove their undoing.

5

Magical Thinking

If there is a ground zero for the intellectual insurgency that propelled Donald Trump back into office, it sits on Massachusetts Avenue, a brisk walk from the White House, behind an eight-storey neoclassical façade of pale sandstone and grey that projects all the institutional gravitas of a Washington think tank.

The Heritage Foundation, once the nerve centre of Ronald Reagan conservatism, has recast itself as the command post for Project 2025 – a sprawling blueprint, hundreds of pages long, to remake America's government in the image of the populist right and the closest thing the President had to a manifesto. When I arrived one humid afternoon in the Washington spring, the pavement outside was blocked by a small and furious knot of protesters. We were whisked through the back door up the stairs and into the grandeur of the Krieble Boardroom: part corporate sanctum, part library, thickly carpeted, its dark wood polished to an ox-blood sheen. Heritage does not hide its heritage; in the corner by the window, like a reliquary in the side chapel of a medieval cathedral, sits Margaret Thatcher's writing desk. And in a way, that was why I was here. Because to understand why populists are winning, I had to understand how somehow they have brokered a marriage of protectionist nostalgia and libertarian freedom. How can populists preach true liberty as gospel yet trade levies as policy? Can populists really promise both factories reborn and freedoms unbound? What, I wondered, is the magical thinking that reconciles two conflicting promises of protection for producers and tariffs at the frontier with a world free of rules for cyberspace?

Nostalgia and the hunger for something lost is the third great power chord of populist rhetoric uncovered in our analysis. Indeed, this is such an important sentiment in American populism, it has become the basis of the new administration's revolutionary approach to trade, upending the free-trading order that a generation of American leaders helped to build. But this economics of nostalgia – what I call nostronomics – is the very antithesis of the libertarian, free-trading tradition that Thatcher championed in office and that today appears still to inspire the futurism of the tech bros who paid for President Trump's election.

In the populist speeches we studied, notions of nostalgia are vivid and consistent – they harmonise with both the themes of patriotism and renewal, and the urgent summons to action. In the speech patterns around nostalgia we see the words we might expect: an invocation of nation or nationality to emphasise a call to return to the 'prior nation' along with words like 'back' (as in 'take back' or 'get back'). The narrative is familiar – a necessary restoration of the past – and when we study the clusters of topics populists extol, we find a fascinating obsession with time. They deploy bundles of words and phrases about time past and future, along with terms denoting time frames both immediate – 'today', 'now', 'yesterday', 'tomorrow', 'week', 'year', 'decades' – and historical, like 'past', 'future', 'already' and 'recently'. 'Time' is a device populist leaders use to frame narratives of decline and nostalgia, offering a contrast between past, present and a potential future. And, by situating issues in time, populist leaders create a sense of immediacy and urgency for change: so words like 'today' and 'now' imply that challenges are pressing while references to 'years' and 'centuries' enlarge the stakes, evoking the notion that national identity and struggle are part of a long historical arc. So, a yearning for the past and a call for restoration is delivered with a rhetorical strategy that underscores both the urgency of the moment, an idealised past and a sense that the future can be different.

Like everything else in the populist song-book, these ideals have a resonance in the depths of human psychology. Long before parliaments and prime ministers, our survival on the prehistoric savannah demanded we tread carefully between risk and ruin by learning from those who went before us; whether it was picking the berries we knew wouldn't kill us or following the hunting routes that kept the tribe fed. This wisdom of the past has long been a cornerstone of Conservative thinking, which cherishes Herodotus's insight that 'custom is king'. Today an invocation of the past is one of the sheet anchors that moors populists on the right of politics, in the arguments that date back to the first days of Conservative intellectual history. Since the French Revolution, conservative philosophers have done a fine job hardening the yen for the familiar into a creed. So, when the sans-culottes were rattling the parapets of Paris during the French Revolution, Edmund

Burke stood aghast at the folly of tearing down an order without knowing what might rise from the rubble. The wiser course, he declared, was for people to 'avail themselves of the general bank and capital of nations and of ages'.[1] Not so long later, the Savoyard diplomat and Catholic philosopher Joseph de Maistre had something similar to say in the wake of Napoleon's chaos: 'Men never respect what they have made themselves', he wrote; keep alive your institutions, he counselled, for they are 'the work of time.'[2] In the early days of the American republic, Alexis de Tocqueville came to similar conclusions: in 1830s America he found the fountainhead of its democratic experiment not in laws but in religion – 'the first of their political institutions' – binding liberty to virtue.[3]

Because change has accelerated so fast in the last century, Conservative thinkers have leaned heavily on these arguments and in creative ways; from G. K. Chesterton, who advised us never to dismantle a fence until we know why it is there,[4] to Michael Oakeshott, who praised the temperament that 'prefers the familiar to the unknown, the tried to the untried',[5] to Russell Kirk, the American architect of the right's post-war canon, who called custom and continuity 'the result of centuries of trial and reflection and sacrifice',[6] to Roger Scruton, aesthete and defender of the English countryside, who offered a line often cited by Giorgia Meloni: 'Good things are easily destroyed, but not easily created.'[7]

In an age when technology, trade, migration and social media re-shape old ways, old communities, even old language so quickly, tradition is a valuable political currency, a deep-coded reassurance that the world won't change faster than you can live in it. The philosophers saw tradition as a stabiliser. Voters are just following the instinct that when the future looks uncertain you hold on tighter to the past. And populists know it's a vote-winner, which is why we see nostalgia riddled throughout their speeches.

Giorgia Meloni is a good example. She has often praised the influence of philosopher Roger Scruton and her party slogan – Dio, patria e famiglia – 'God, Homeland, Family' is Chesterton's democracy of the dead in campaign-speech form. In her 2019 campaign speech, her paean to the traditions of culture, religion and sex was a viral hit: 'I am Giorgia,' she declared, 'I am a woman, I am a mother, I am Italian, I am Christian … No one will take that away from me.'[8] She echoed this 'cultural conservationist' argument in 2022, arguing that protection of natural heritage 'engages us in exactly the same way as protecting the heritage of culture, traditions, and spirituality that we inherited from our fathers so that we could pass it on to our children'.[9] Because this is a 'civilisational struggle', Meloni sees the battlefront as arcing far wider than merely Italian politics. Speaking to an American audience, she declared in 2025, 'the political and cultural battle for conservative values is not just an American battle. It is a Western battle.'[10] Donald Trump agrees. He argued in Florida in 2022 that 'the Judeo-Christian values and principles of our nation's founding' were 'under assault'.[11]

Nigel Farage, by contrast, makes speeches that are similar but with a subtle difference, arguing from history rather than religion. In 2013, for example, he said: 'Our [British] geography puts us apart. Our history puts us apart. Our institutions produced by that history put us apart. [Hence] We think differently. We behave differently.'[12]

But no one relies on the cult of ancestor worship and the defence of 'Christian Europe' quite as much as Viktor Orbán. Hungary's long-serving prime minister has long claimed Europe is trying to 'forget or eradicate its Christian identity'[13] and offers a more extreme twist on the same theme: 'We believe that the Hungarian spirit can support anything and survive anything. As our ancestors said: "It sometimes loses its voice, but it does not die."'

Ancestors, heritage, history, inheritance, institutions. These are potent story-lines at any time, but at moments of huge economic loss, they acquire a special force. And as community after community has lost the work that was once its dignity, pride and pay, so the yearning for nostronomics has got louder and louder.

Between 2000 and 2016, America lost nearly 5 million manufacturing jobs. Real wages stagnated. Entire regions of industrial America have become deeply, deeply scarred by opioid epidemics, economic decay and political rage, a story narrated with eloquence by the Vice President, J. D. Vance, in *Hillbilly Elegy*: 'The loss of personal dignity that comes from the absence of stable, well-paying employment', he wrote with feeling, 'is not something that can be compensated for by cheap imported goods or welfare checks.'

The Vice President is now at the centre of a knot of 'postliberal' thinkers who share the idea that liberalism – and liberal capitalism – must be retired.[14] Yale Professor Patrick Deneen has written one of the core texts of the argument: 'liberalism needs not reform but retirement',[15] not because it has failed, but because, in his telling, it has succeeded in all the wrong ways in creating a society that 'generates titanic inequality, enforces uniformity and homogeneity, fosters material and spiritual degradation, and undermines freedom',[16] loosening the ties that once bound communities together.[17]

As an honest-to-goodness conservative, Professor Deneen naturally blames over-large governments for much of this but the free market is not spared, not least 'the drive for quick profits ... [which] replaces investment and trusteeship'[18] along with behaviour that fuels both 'the depletion of moral self-command and the depletion of material resources'.[19]

This critique reflects truths that the left would share about the way American capitalism has created modern oligopolies[20] which are so powerful they constitute, in the words of Sohrab Ahmari, a socially conservative former *Wall Street Journal* columnist, 'private tyrannies' in a 'system that allows the asset-owning few to subject the asset-less many to pervasive coercion'. Nor is this simply an American problem. In his book on Europe, Christopher Caldwell deplored the way market liberalism 'that accords no particular value to Europe's most cherished traditions'[21] was amongst the forces that now spell 'a permanent and undesirable cultural alteration of their continent'.[22]

This sort of jeremiad has a long tradition in American politics. But this is no longer a mere lament for something lost. It is now an inspiration for the future of American policy – and President Trump's shock therapy for the global trade system.

Ideas take time to change politics. And the master theorist of this revolution is no longer a young man. Robert Lighthizer is a litigator with the patience of a chess player. Trump's first US Trade Representative, he was the architect of the President's first trade war, and is now the spiritual godfather of today's second act. For decades, he sat in the shadows while free trade defined the Washington Consensus. Now, with President Trump's return, the nostrums of his long game are the executive orders of the day, and his arguments – tariffs as weapons, sovereignty as strategy, compromise as surrender – define Washington's daily discourse. For Lighthizer, America's free-trade policy was not only flawed, it was betrayal: 'American leaders traded the health of the US industrial base and the good-paying manufacturing jobs it supported for current consumption and little more', he railed in his book *No Trade is Free*. Free trade, Lighthizer argues, was never real: 'Free trade is a unicorn – a figment of the Anglo-American imagination. No one really believes in it outside of countries in the Anglo-American world, and no one practices it.'

That is the thinking that now inspires the architects of President Trump's nostronomics, and it can be found in two buildings 250 yards apart in Washington DC. Looming over the White House, the Eisenhower Executive Office Building stands like a gothic fortress on Pennsylvania Avenue, all stone columns, iron balconies, and imperial swagger. Mark Twain called it 'the ugliest building in Washington'. Here is the home to the economists, the lawyers, the national-security hawks, the architects of economic war. Inside, power is drafted, redlined, offered up as orders for the President. And here is the home of the Council of Economic Advisers, formerly chaired by Stephen Miran, whom I met in the CEA's meeting room, its walls decked with the photographs of Council chairs dating back decades, and tall windows affording agreeable views of the White House.

Mr Miran, a former senior adviser at the US Treasury under Trump, is kind, courteous and clever and one of the intellectual architects behind the new tariff state. If you're looking for the theory of today's shock therapy, you would best turn to his 2024 essay 'The Mar-a-Lago Accord', in which he argued that America must abandon free-trade orthodoxy and rebuild national manufacturing strength through 'strategic re-industrialization'.

The vision, on paper, is arrestingly simple: a supply-side push to deliver growth without inflation. Re-shore manufacturing. Tilt the trade field level. Boost exports. Cut tax and red tape. Unleash cheap energy. In Stephen Miran's words, it is nothing less than the recovery of something squandered: 'We are moving beyond free trade. We are building economic sovereignty.'

For three decades, he argues, America 'offshored everything to China and let Wall Street price American labour'. Now the order is reversed: bring the factories home, rebuild the base, repatriate dignity with jobs.

Two hundred and fifty yards across the street, in the HQ of the US Trade Representative, they are tasked with turning theory into practice. Like a relic from the early days of the Republic, the Winder Building squats on 17th Street. Its lacquered red-brick floors, elegant curved balconies and clunky lifts have seen over a century and a half of American power games. Behind its unassuming doors, the US Trade Representative helps run the nerve centre of America's economic wars, haggling the new rules of the world trading system. The TV in reception is tuned to Fox News. Beneath it someone has written a little notice in marker pen on a scrap of cardboard: 'Do Not Change the Channel'.

'We are faced with a situation where the US has a trade deficit of over a trillion dollars,' one official tells me. 'That's the largest by any country at any time in history. That type of trade deficit is unsustainable.'

And here they are crystal clear about the culprits: 'The reason for this trade imbalance isn't due to natural market outcomes but to non-market policies and practices by other countries massively subsidising their industries and flooding world markets.' Especially China. Now that must change.

For many allies in the blast radius of this new policy, however, the daily negotiations feel, as one European diplomat put it to me in London, like a 'shakedown'. 'It's not just America First, but it's making everyone pay, making the rest of the world pay in order to put America first ... how much can we get you to pay us to leave you alone.'

Right now, politicians around the world find it hard to understand exactly what the American objective might be. Is it to fix the trade balance? Grow the economy? Keep inflation and interest rates low? Re-shore manufacturing? In fact it is all of these things. But especially the last one. The USTR's objective, I was told in no uncertain terms, 'is that when [Trump] leaves office, US manufacturing as a share of GDP and employment will have risen'. Whatever the economics of nostalgia, whatever the cost to the West, American populists are determined to relieve America's hunger for something lost with a restoration of the industries that powered the past.

Freedom and futurism

The challenge of nostronomics is how to reconcile a restoration of lost industry with a restoration of the freedom that populists argue went missing as the global economy was built. Freedom is important to populists. When we probe what exactly populists say is lost, 'freedom', and 'right(s)' are the words we see most often co-occurring. In speeches outside the UK this reference to 'freedom' and 'rights' often co-occurs with conservatism (or 'conservative'). Another 'topic-cluster' buttresses the appeal, freighted with emotion and moral weight by words like 'liberty', 'justice', 'truth', 'hope', 'dream' and 'courage'.

Take, for example, President Trump's second inaugural address: 'Now it is our time to take up the righteous cause of American liberty', he declared. Or look at the words of Giorgia Meloni: 'Freedom is the foundation of a true society of opportunity; it is freedom that must guide our actions, freedom to be, to do, to produce. A centre-right government will never restrict the existing freedoms of citizens and businesses ... Freedom. Freedom and democracy are the distinctive elements of contemporary European civilization ...'[23]

Marine Le Pen's speeches offer a similar tale: 'The third pillar of our project is freedom. For several years, everyone has felt that a sort of lid has been placed on society. Political correctness forces adherence to the tyranny of conformity.'[24] Nor is it hard to find British parallels. Here is Richard Tice MP, in a speech to the Reform UK conference in 2023: 'The zealots, the cultists in this new religion, want us to change our cars. They want us to change our boilers. They want us to travel less. They don't want us to eat delicious wonderful succulent steaks. They want to change everything and we need to tell them that the answer is no, and be under no illusion voters across Europe are now rebelling and revolting against this appalling madness.'[25]

Freedom has been long important to Conservative ideology and, in recent years, this story has been electrified, if not digitalised, by an update to the libertarian tradition delivered by a community that invested hundreds of millions of dollars in President Trump's re-election. The 'techno-libertarians'[26] bring to the table a sizzling mix of sci-fi vision, libertarian thinking, billions of dollars, and the social skills of pampered teenage boys who have spent too much time alone in their bedrooms. Many appear haunted, as one critic put it, with the 'growing sense of social frustration among mostly white, middle-class males resentful of diminished economic and social fortunes in a diverse, economically slowing, post-Third Wave feminist society'.[27]

On their bedroom floors could be found dog-eared copies of Ayn Rand's libertarian novels like *Atlas Shrugged*, written through with her philosophy that 'selfishness is a virtue', along with Seattle-born Neal Stephenson's *Snow Crash*, the dystopian novel that imagines a balkanised America where the federal government has withered, replaced by corporate city-states, franchised power, anarchic digital realms, outsourced law and order and instead 'of one nation under God, there were hundreds of little nation-states under a dozen different gods'.[28]

The techno-libertarians have three core issues – extreme privacy, extreme free speech and cryptocurrency. They derive from a small cluster of potent ideas that flow from early work of John Perry Barlow, whose manifesto, 'A Declaration of the Independence of Cyberspace' declared: 'Governments have no place in cyberspace.' In this new world, information is the ultimate currency of power. Once upon a time, government held almost a monopoly on information but new technology like cryptography would, it was argued, erode this, letting people transact and communicate outside traditional oversight. From this follows the idea that code might one day replace many of the functions performed by public institutions, allowing them to be rebuilt as open, decentralised networks. Smart-contract theorists like Nick Szabo extended the argument further: agreements could execute themselves without courts or officials, and trust could be anchored in mathematics rather than authority. In these decentralised systems, no one single actor – like the state – was needed to supply and enforce trust. In the end, writers like Vernor Vinge concluded that accelerating technological change might render existing political systems obsolete altogether. The brave new world would not be a place with much need for states or governments anymore.

Populism and techno-libertarianism are not the same. One is a movement of the masses, the other a creed of the coders. Yet they share a common contempt for central authority – the gospel Steve Bannon preached in Trumpworld. A former US naval officer, Goldman Sachs banker, and media executive, Bannon rose to prominence as head of Breitbart News before becoming Donald Trump's chief strategist in the White House – a post he lost after just seven months in 2017. But his gospel returned to centre stage when President Trump, 'under considerable pressure from this group', named J. D. Vance, long a disciple of Peter Thiel, as his running mate. And the sermon grew louder when Elon Musk poured millions into Trump's re-election, bought Twitter, scrapped 'nearly all moderation' and enthroned himself as chief troll. The result was a strange new hybrid: an alt-right spectacle fused with accelerationist techno-utopianism – the very cocktail mixed for years by Mr Thiel and his friends.

Quite how the tariff-warriors and tech-libertarians are going to get on is anyone's guess. For now, the President Trump has kept them, by and large, on the same ship. But only magical thinking could allow you to believe that somehow there is a complete unity of purpose. When I met the Heritage Foundation, I had hoped to discover the secret to this reconciliation. I was left with the clear sense that, philosophically at least, there has been no reconciliation. I had come expecting a fluent defence of the President's nostronomics and the case for rebuilding what American communities had lost. Maybe even a justification for a new Great Wall of America sealing the nation off so towns wrecked by the free-trading economics of the last Washington Consensus could be reborn. I didn't get it. As the Heritage team admitted, trade strategy was so fraught it needed 'one chapter which is protectionist [and] one chapter that's free trade'. This was the price of building a coalition of more than 120 organisations ranging from free-marketeers to 'the ultimate protectionist' camp, the kind who 'would turn this country economically into North Korea if they could'. The result? No clear road-map, just factions – and the unspoken truth that, as one participant put it, 'it doesn't always help to rationalise crazy'. Not a plan. A truce.

How might the populists' magical thinking remain intact? How do populists think they will ride the two horses of extreme freedom and an end to free trade? The populists appear to be selling a promise which is tough to keep: yesterday's factories, tomorrow's freedoms. The question is not whether this is popular. The question is whether it is possible.

Populists offer only a single blueprint: let a strong leader work it out. Do not leave it to messy, vote-counting democracies. The 'post-Liberals' and techno-libertarians may come from opposite ends of the cultural highway, but they share two big reflexes – one obvious, the other more surprising. Both deprecate deep states, big governments, and, of course, 'faceless global elites'. But they are equally disenchanted with democracy, and in some cases, go as far as to advocate for monarchy.

In 2014, *The Baffler* wryly observed that tech bros' enthusiasm for monarchies sprang from never having 'to play the part of the peasant'.[29] In fact, the authoritarian populist disaffection with democracy has been growing for some years. At the turn of the century, Hans-Hermann Hoppe's *Democracy: The God That Failed*,[30] which became an autho-pop bible, listed a long indictment of democracy's sins: immigration, rising crime rates, the erosion of personal responsibility, an 'abundance of tolerance'. From there, the table of crimes simply lengthened – taxation, the welfare state, public ownership. Democracy therefore had to go, said Hoppe, because it was 'ultimately destroying Western civilization, values and economic prosperity'. Monarchy, in this telling, is better: 'because a monarch can rule with longer term goals and more legitimacy for their decisions … under democratic conditions the popular, if immoral and anti-social, desire for other men's property is systematically strengthened.'

You might think these arguments are on the fringe and for many years they were. But within a decade Peter Thiel – billionaire, monopoly-defender and major backer of both President Trump and Vice-President Vance – was echoing the sentiment, albeit in an essay he later disavowed: 'I no longer believe that freedom and democracy are compatible.'[31] Mr Thiel sketched a world where innovation, not elections, picks the winners: 'One of the things I like about technology is that when technology's un-regulated you can change the world without getting approval from other people. At its best, it's not subject to democratic control, and not subject to the majority, which I think is often hostile to change.'

These arguments are not over. Indeed, their evangelists are very much in fashion. Few are so eye-catching as Curtis Yarvin, friend of the Vice President and better known as the blogger Moldbug, who weds radical libertarianism to authoritarianism, and promotes maximum personal freedom in everything except politics. Dismissing elections – 'Elections give the illusion of responding to social demands,' he wrote, 'but are false safety valves that mask progressive control' – his prescription is for an elected CEO-monarch to rule for the 'shareholders' of the state.

In better times we might dismiss all this as 'on the fringe'. But given what we know of authoritarian populists in power, that would be a mistake. Patriotism. Nostalgia. Struggle. These are not incidental themes. They are powerful forces with hard edges, delivered with conversational ease. While mainstream politicians talk in policies, populists talk in parables. While mainstreamers are planners, populists are preachers.

And the sermon is simple.

We are told the past can be recovered.

We are told the future can be unfettered.

We are told one leader can deliver both.

Surely we should ask, *How?* Henry Kissinger once observed that 'democracies evolve in a conflict of factions. They achieve greatness by their reconciliations'. It is too early to tell whether today's populists can reconcile the nostalgia of the 'good ole boys' of rural America with the futurism of the tech bros of Silicon Valley. For now they hold the coalition in uneasy balance – enough to govern, and above all to communicate with incredible effect – using one crucial force to which we now turn: the populist social-media machine.

6

Engage and Enrage

When Demosthenes, the Greek master of rhetoric, was asked for the secret of his success, he had but a three-word answer: 'Delivery, delivery, delivery.'[1] Mastering the means of communication has always been the key, the x factor, to landing your point, and what was true in the agora of ancient Greece is true in the arenas of modern politics. Which is why we cannot decode why populists are winning without a close study of the way populists dominate the modern medium of social media, built with three simple features – visible metrics, algorithmic ranking, and one-click sharing – which underwrite a partnership with outrage.

Across the Western world, social media has become our principal gateway to the news – already ahead of TV in America,[2] it is the main source of news for four in ten of us in Europe.[3] On these new digital channels, populist politicians radically outperform their mainstream rivals because they share with the social-media firms the logic of outrage. In the past, the old guardrails – the editor's red pen, the broadcaster's duty of balance – damped incendiary rhetoric. Now they are gone; the outrage that animates the populist message is the outrage that platforms are tuned to accelerate. Populists and platforms share a business model: while populists politicise anger, fear and threat, social media firms commercialise anger, fear and threat. One seeks to mobilise, the other seeks to monetise. One seeks votes, the other seeks profits. But both seek power.

As we saw in Chapter 4, populists conjure this anger and perception of threat by summoning the quintessence of the populist appeal; the idea of struggle against newcomers, novelty and difference. This is calculated pathos. As researchers have long understood, perception of threat is the pre-eminent trigger that activates authoritarian predispositions. Not merely physical threat, but 'threats to the moral order'.[4] Well, as it turns out, the same dark materials are exactly the sort of content that social-media firms need to hold and monetise your attention.

Attention has long been valuable. In his book,[5] Columbia University professor Tim Wu dates the emergence of 'attention merchants' back to the first ad-driven penny papers of nineteenth-century New York, the commercial artists of Paris,[6] and the propagandists and recruiters of the First World War. But over the course of the twentieth century, the sophistication of the global ad industry transformed us from mere impressionable consumers to what Wu christens 'homo distractus' – 'a species of ever greater and ever shorter attention spans, known for compulsively checking devices'[7] – and the attention merchants have become some of the most valuable firms on earth; the digital advertising industry now has a worldwide value of $790 billion.[8] Ad sales make up 98 per cent of Meta's revenue, 77 per cent of TikTok's and 68 per cent of X's.[9]

To create this value, social media platforms have been built by some of the smartest people on the planet to optimise for one core metric – engagement.[10] In almost no time at all, firms discovered that three bits of engineering were essential: visible social metrics (likes, shares, follower counts), algorithmic ranking of feeds, and one-click sharing. Together these features shift your feed from a boring old chronological order to predicted reaction, privileging content that provokes fast, emotional responses over slower, reflective reading. The design owes much to the science of behavioural reinforcement – variable, intermittent rewards attached to metrics ('how many liked this?') – and conditions users to create the kinds of posts that previously drew interaction. Recommendation systems then fetch more of whatever elicits those reactions in similar users.

Two dynamics amplify the effect. First, emotional contagion: feelings expressed in posts are mirrored by others, creating cascades of similar emotion at scale. Second, network formation around homophily: group-finding tools and recommender systems cluster like-minded users, increasing the supply of agreeable material and the probability of rapid reshares.

In this attention refinery, borderline posts – provocative yet policy-compliant – receive disproportionate lift. Context collapses into a clip which then spreads as as resharers add new frames; trigger-chains follow, pushing the controversial through feeds. These mechanics have symmetrical outcomes. Entertainment travels efficiently: humour, novelty and awe are highly shareable and receive algorithmic lift. But the same dynamics spread more divisive material. Entertainment scales but so does enmity.

Early studies of viral posts discovered quickly that tweets with 'moral and emotional' content spread much faster;[11]

Facebook posts containing 'indignant disagreement' were found to be more widely shared and commented on,[12] and false news, rich in novelty value, was 70 per cent more likely to be shared than true stories.[13] As creators receive positive feedback for posts that trigger stronger reactions, 'audience capture' nudges content strategies towards sharper tones. And because attention translates into advertising value, there is a commercial incentive to produce material – across news, politics and brands – that reliably stimulates interaction. The simple lesson is that moral-emotional language increases diffusion, whilst novelty and shock guarantee more success than correctness.

At system level, these dynamics reshape discourse rather than merely reflect it. By ranking for predicted engagement, feeds tilt towards conflict-salient items; by clustering similar users, they reduce incidental exposure to alternative frames; by rewarding provocation, they expand the salience of extreme proposals and pull the Overton window towards the edges. What emerges from this digital Darwinism is infrastructure that efficiently spreads both delight and disgust, entertainment and enmity, according to the same optimisation logic: maximise measurable reaction, and then supply more of what reacts.

Put it all together, and you have what MIT professor Sinan Aral calls a 'hype machine'.[14] 'How do they get engagement?' asks Aral. 'Well, they give you little dopamine hits, and ... get you riled up. That's why I call it the hype machine. We know strong emotions get us engaged, so [that favors] anger and salacious content.'[15] In his superb book, technologist and media researcher Tobias Rose-Stockwell goes further. Social media is no longer merely a hype machine, he declares. It is an outrage machine and helping fuel its furnaces is a cottage industry of 'rage-tainment' producers. These producers include the politicians desperate for likes in the hope that likes mean votes.

A short history of sensationalism

Yet, hasn't it been ever thus? Over 2,000 years ago, Aristotle wrote in *Rhetoric* that persuasion always requires a hefty dose of pathos.[16] The tug of emotion – values, shared hopes, fear – is always required if a speaker wants to move an audience to action. As technology advanced, so the medium of the media magnified the sensational. As literacy spread and technology changed, entrepreneurs like Lord Northcliffe, William Randolph Hearst and Joseph Pulitzer harnessed telegraphs, steam-powered rotary presses, wood-pulp paper and linotype machines to create the first tabloids and, with it, the 'yellow journalism' of aggressive reporting, sensational headlines, emotive language and plenty of crime and death. 'Shock and amaze on every page' was the editor's rule of thumb; 'if it bleeds, it leads'. Radio gave demagogues a microphone. Cinema newsreels gave fascists a stage. Television brought the combative talk shows of Joe Pyne and Jerry Springer. Cable news turned crisis into rolling spectacle. Each innovation shortened the fuse between stimulus and response. Each made politics more about performance than policy.

Yet throughout that long history, politicians on the right side of fascism observed the basic boundaries of decency. Think of the stagecraft and set pieces of the newsreels, the conversational fireside chats of Franklin Roosevelt, the vividness of Churchill's radio rhetoric or the civility of the first Nixon and Kennedy TV debates. Even the spin culture of the 1990s was rarely vicious every day. The advent of digital media changed all this; it lit the way for the 'enrage and rule' style of modern populism. The populists' digital pathos did not appear out of nowhere. Its methods date to some lessons learned from a surprising inspiration: the Italian Marxist Antonio Gramsci.

Gramsci's heirs

A brilliant scholar, Antonio Gramsci was born in Sardinia and graduated from the University of Turin before becoming a prominent organiser, editor and soon leader of the Italian Communist Party. Imprisoned by Mussolini in 1926, Gramsci used his time inside to write his *Prison Notebooks*,[17] in which emerged the notion that power is not merely held by coercion but through consent manufactured and sustained by a nation's institutions. Power, argued Gramsci, isn't simply wielded by those with tanks or a seat in the boardroom but by those who write the story we all think we live in. Rulers rule when their worldview feels like the common sense of daily life. To break the mould, *the hegemony*, argued Gramsci, a movement therefore required its own storytellers, 'organised intellectuals' in a counterculture strong enough to win a 'war of position'. It was less about storming palace gates than about rewiring the minds.

The idea was profoundly influential with early populists like French thinker Alain de Benoist and the Nouvelle Droite, a new group of intellectual entrepreneurs who abandoned the old street-fighting militancy of the French far right and turned to their typewriters to pioneer a 'metapolitics' of their own. De Benoist and his fellow travellers in the Research and Study Group for European Civilization (GRECE) realised that Gramsci had been right: in advanced societies, transitions occur, not through coups or revolutions but 'through the transformation of general ideas that amounts to a slow remolding of minds'.[18] By 1981 GRECE was organising conferences with snappy names like 'For a right wing Gramscianism'[19] and, by the early 1990s, the American paleoconservatives were onto the idea. Samuel Francis, a sharp-tongued columnist turned ideological arsonist who railed against multiculturalism and global elites long before President Trump made it fashionable, was among the first to argue for a cultural struggle, advising his readers that if 'the cultural right in the US is to take back its culture from those who have usurped it, it will find a study of Gramsci's ideas rewarding'.[20] That year, Pat Buchanan announced his America First challenge for the American presidency. Writing later in his manifesto, *The Death of the West*, Buchanan reprised his thinking: 'it's the culture, stupid!'[21] He denounced 'political correctness' as 'cultural Marxism', declared 'America has become an ideological state' and railed against the 'soft tyranny where the new orthodoxy is enforced not by police agents, but by the inquisitors of popular culture'.

Strategically, the early populists knew, as de Benoist had long argued, that victory required their movement 'to position the radical right as a plausible partner to the working class',[22] yet tactically they knew that their best chance of a breakthrough was to find a way to go direct. The influential argument-maker Murray Rothbard, an anarcho-capitalist economist and early co-founder of the Cato Institute, was very clear-eyed: populists needed to 'short circuit the media elites and reach and rouse the masses directly'.[23] But at the time, the populists could not reach beyond the daytime talk-radio shock jocks like Rush Limbaugh and Howard Stern. The revolution in cable, code and clickbait changed all that.

Fox News, launched in 1996 in New York by Republican strategist Roger Ailes, backed by media mogul Rupert Murdoch, soon perfected a format that blended news and partisan opinion in a single output, smothering current affairs in the emotional cadence of talk radio and the intimacy of daytime TV. By the mid-2000s, it had become a kingmaker in Republican primaries, an agenda-setter for the White House.

Facebook had humbler roots. Crafted from a couple of thousand lines of code by Mark Zuckerberg between classes at Harvard, within six years it became the largest social network on the planet and, like Fox News, it soon proved that anger travelled an awful lot faster than accuracy. Its news feed became a new front page for millions of people, curated not by editors, but by the cold arithmetic of clicks and comments. Twitter was two years younger but just as potent. With a canvas of merely 140 characters, it stripped argument down to the barest bones without the fat of context. Within six years, it boasted 200 million users and became the real-time wire service for politics worldwide, a place where journalists sourced stories, politicians broke news and movements were born in hashtags. But by collapsing time and space, it collapsed reflection, rewarded provocation, punished nuance and turned political life into a permanent performance. It was perfect for the populist politician. The advent of TikTok reshaped the battlefield once again. Launched in 2017, it featured more entertainment than news but its impact took logic to an extreme: filters gave way to algorithms that personalised your feed to attention triggers you never knew you had.

Fox perfected a tone. Facebook perfected targeting. Twitter perfected speed and TikTok perfected the hook. Together these channels have transformed the way that populists cut through. Populists are far more effective on social media than mainstream leaders for the simple reason that they are masters of the methods that are rewarded. And so we find ourselves in a world where, the more we connect, the less we converge.

It was not long before studies revealed populist parties were outperforming mainstream parties because their content – emotional, conflict-framed, video-first and voluminous – was exactly what social media's outrage engineering was designed to spread. In Italy, the most Facebook-frenzied nation in Europe, Lega's Matteo Salvini was soon posting 35 times a day – 20 times the European average.[24] In France, Belgium and the Netherlands, the most populist parties were the most vociferous keyboard warriors. And they were successful. By 2015 the average UKIP Facebook post was already drawing 4,000 'Likes' – twice the number of a post from the Conservative Party. Germany's AfD had twice the Facebook following of Angela Merkel.[25]

More recent algorithm audits show systematic amplification of right-leaning political content on X/Twitter, mixed evidence for YouTube recommendations, and growing concerns about TikTok. On the House of Commons'

Joint Committee on National Security Strategy, we have been taking a close interest in this. Evidence from one expert at Oxford University stayed with me: 'While designed to enhance user engagement,' wrote Professor Dabbagh, 'algorithms often inadvertently amplify divisive content, fostering echo chambers and reinforcing extreme viewpoints'[26].

In six out of seven countries studied, Twitter's algorithm was found to disproportionately amplify right-leaning political content compared to left-leaning content,[27] while in Germany researchers found that TikTok's algorithm was disproportionally amplifying the far-right AfD.[28,29]

But is there more to the populists' playbook than this? To help us understand this, we invited Alison Phillips, a groundbreaking editor of the British tabloid the *Daily Mirror*, along with the founder of Conservative Home – and new Reform member – Tim Montgomerie, to St Anthony's College in Oxford for a discussion on the future of the media in the age of populism.[30]

Alison began by decoding the secret of populists' social-media success, which apparently begins by turning up in the places where citizens happen to live their cultural lives.

'The trick, I think, to Donald Trump's success is that while so many Democrats and politicians generally work and operate in a news space, populists play in that much, much greater entertainment space where actually most of the public live their lives. That's why he's focused on things like WWE wrestling … That is where people spend their time. They want to be entertained. And great populists are great entertainers.'

They combine this, Alison argues, with a 'vivid ability to tell stories. Populist communication is all about emotion.

It's about content which makes you really angry, makes you cry, or makes you laugh, which essentially was the basis for all sensationalist journalism. Whereas, unfortunately, people on the left particularly, tend to be more interested in data and facts and graphs.'

This instinct for entertainment, now labelled 'politainment' in media-studies circles – is something populists take seriously. Indeed, back in 2017, the *New York Times* reported that President Trump had instructed his staff, 'to think of each presidential day as an episode in a television show in which he vanquishes his rivals'.[31]

'Great storytelling', Phillips went on, 'is about ... playing in a moral place where you can talk about moral stories and engage people on a human level. And [populists] combine it with authenticity. In any great stories, you've got to feel the person who's told you understands you. They feel for you.'

But populists owe their success to more than mastery of social-media algorithms. They are winning because the foundation stone of public debate – trust in news – has now cracked beneath our feet. The numbers tell a brutal story. According to Reuters,[32] just 40 per cent of people across 47 countries say they trust the news. In Britain, it's just 36 per cent. Indeed, things are now so bad that almost half the population (46 per cent) say they actively avoid the news, a figure that has doubled in just eight years.

As Alison explained, British media has hardly helped itself. From the paparazzi pursuit of Princess Diana to the hacking of phones of private citizens, the British media has a sorry history that has corroded public faith. Editorial newsrooms and their leaders were drawn from the same narrow social pool with a narrowed perspective that failed to forecast Brexit, the rise of Jeremy Corbyn and the possibility of President Trump's election.

The economics of today's media makes the challenge greater because the sheer cost of what traditional media did best – good old-fashioned forensic investigations – is so much harder to afford. In Britain, Google and Facebook have now captured around 90 per cent of digital ad revenue, destroying the sales of traditional media and their ability to finance the old investigative craft. Democracy's immune system is depleting and degrading. But at the same time, a flood tide of information, disinformation and misinformation is surging, and a crisis of trust is becoming a crisis of truth as, in the vast wilderness of content, nobody knows what to believe anymore.

These techniques were perfected by the Russians, who were quick to understand the potential of the 'firehose of falsehood':[33] if there is enough conflict, truths, half-truths and lies in the mix, no one will know anything for sure. A 'post-truth' world is exactly where populists like to live. It not only allows them to escape scrutiny, it also hands an advantage to both their A-listers and affinities, who, together with AI-driven algorithms, can take someone on a conveyor belt from open-minded tolerance to hardcore conspiracy theories in a remarkably short space of time.

The populist A-lister is a new but essential component of the system. It is an old truth that the thicker the jungle the more important the guide. For decades now, what Tim Wu calls the celebrity entertainment complex has created personalities with cosmic cut-through, from Oprah Winfrey to Elon Musk. But when personalities own platforms, platforms can own the narrative.

One of the organisers of the Cambridge Disinformation Summit at Cambridge University,[34] Professor Alan Jagolinzer, a former US Air Force pilot and now business-school professor, explained it to me like this: 'We are now in the most acute information and accountability crisis of our lifetime', and for evidence he pointed simply at the power of Elon Musk to set a political agenda. In early January 2025, Musk had decided to weigh into the UK debate on the need for an inquiry into the terrible case of grooming children for sex. The Prime Minister had set out a way forward – but Musk attacked it. 'Musk just puts forty tweets, forty tweets', Alan exploded, 'and the entire news media here spent a good chunk of a week only on that. I cannot say this loudly enough. Musk hijacked the entire narrative around the UK for about six days. With forty tweets.'

If you're a populist politician with an A-list influencer on your side, you've got a head start in today's world, especially if they own the platform and have refined its algorithms in ways that somehow end up delivering a super-sized serving of populist tropes to innocent users. Bad actors like President Putin used to have to create entire 'bot factories' filled with people creating 'sock puppet' accounts to spread and share divisive content. Now there are accusations that some social media channels have altered their algorithms to key into the semantic content of right-wing messages and amplify it, either directly or indirectly. Hence extreme voices like the AfD in Germany or the far-right activist Tommy Robinson in Britain suddenly find themselves aided and abetted not by the invisible hand of the marketplace but the deliberate hand of the algorithm.

But affinities are just as powerful. Social-media systems are hugely effective at entangling us in like-minded communities of grievance that populists or their proxies can effectively radicalise. Amongst the most insidious today is the 'manosphere', the subject of a recent book by someone I have long admired, the journalist James Bloodworth.

The manosphere is not somewhere I know. So I asked James to explain it to me. The manosphere, he patiently explained, is 'a group of anti-feminist subcultures … that's the simplest way to put it, male supremacist subcultures, [and] anti-feminism is the kind of thing that unites all of the manosphere groups'. In essence it is an exploitative place because at its dark centre it is a hustle, a bazaar where the sellers exploit men's insecurities. As James points out, you can measure its spread by how its tropes now seep into the discourse of Gen Z men. And the bridge to populism, James argues, is structural: 'there's a … similarity in the narrative structure … it's very much about discrediting the mainstream, [and] reverse[ing] the … oppressor, [then] selling themselves as the saviours with the hidden knowledge'. And of course both the manosphere and modern populism, James explained, have something else in common: 'both movements are dominated by essentially charismatic charlatans … the people who thrive in the new media landscape tend to be charismatic, a bit narcissistic, [and] very good at self-promotion', communicating through short, emotive clips and normalising voices once dismissed as fringe.

Two significant risks emerge from these trends. First, the way we consume news and information becomes shaped by what has become known as 'tribal epistemology'. David

Roberts, the originator of the phrase, explains it like this: 'Information is evaluated based not on conformity to common standards of evidence or correspondence to a common understanding of the world, but on whether it supports the tribe's values and goals …'[35] You believe the things you think someone like you should believe.

To an extent this has always been true, as Alison Phillips reminded us: 'Tribalism has always existed in this country. And people have always had their echo chambers. People who bought the *Daily Mirror* bought it because they knew it was going to come with a left-wing view, just as people bought the *Telegraph* because they were right-wing. So those things have always existed.' But we managed to find some common ground, not least because we had greater exposure to real life at work, or in a social life around schools, pubs, bingo halls and sports where people with very different views came together. When we lack this shared community context, we increase the likelihood of some people becoming isolated and subsequently radicalised much faster than before. I learned this from a surprising source.

It was by accident that I discovered that the best political psychologists aren't to be found in Parliament, the gutter press or the ivory towers of the nation's universities. In fact they work for MI5, where, some years ago, I had the chance to meet some of the behavioural-science team.

Radicalisation, they explained, is like a game of snakes and ladders. Things happen that take people to the threshold of violence before, generally speaking, the better angels of our nature prevail. The dynamics are as complicated as humans are unique, but there are patterns. First, there are the 'push factors': the twists of fate, like a dysfunctional family, a personal crisis or some sort of grievance; anything that knocks away restraint to anti-social behaviour. Then there are the 'pull' factors or 'radicalising influences'. These might be family members, close friends, or – more commonly these days – radicalisers found online. But extreme behaviour requires more than a push and pull. It requires rage, a 'switch', a 'shock', an 'ideological opening'. It could be a single event, it could be exposure to a particular cause; whatever it is, it provides a connection to meaning typically expressed as some great redemptive conflict. That is exactly what, at its worst, radical right-wing populists are up to, as the recent riots illustrate all too well.

On 29 July 2024, three young girls were senselessly murdered by Axel Rudakubana at a Taylor Swift-themed party. The appalling crime instantly horrified the nation. Yet before the suspect's name or religion was even known, a torrent of online disinformation ignited riots outside asylum centres across the country. The Home Office later concluded that the 'online environment' was a significant factor in the violence, and a Commons select committee found that 'misleading and hateful messaging proliferated rapidly online, amplified by the recommendation engines of social media companies'.[36] The scale was staggering: false claims about the Southport attacker reached 155 million impressions on X, while a fabricated name circulated in posts with a potential reach of 1.7 billion. Worse, the outrage was monetised. In the week after the attack, right-wing influencers pulled in nearly 40 million ad impressions – generating almost £28,000. A day. Hate not only spread. Hate paid.

IRL

How worried should we be? As part of my research with Best for Britain, I studied how Reform-curious voters in the UK now consume news. There is clearly a generational divide but our polling found that at least a third (33 per cent) of those considering Reform UK pick television as their main news source. Traditional sources remain an anchor for many – especially older audiences – though these are often accessed in digital form. Tabloids such as the *Mail*, *Sun* and *Mirror*, local press like the *Manchester Evening News*, and national TV outlets including the BBC and Sky News are staples, and right-leaning challengers such as TalkTV and GB News make occasional appearances.

But beyond TV, Reform-curious voters are big social-media users,[37] and in this fragmented, hybrid media landscape the lines between news, opinion and entertainment now blur. In this world trust is a rare commodity, including trust in the BBC. As one Midlands man put it, 'The BBC news app, it's been my chosen go-to for a long time ... but I tend to sort of draw my own conclusions, or take everything with a pinch of salt, to say the least.'

Regardless, new voices are now cutting through. On X, Facebook and especially YouTube, there is now an entire alternative news environment. Here you can find channels like Rebel News, Valuetainment and independent commentators who blend documentary formats with sharp editorialising. These 'shockateurs' and 'ragetainment' sources like Rebel News, Channel 5 (Andrew Callaghan), Valuetainment and Hell City all supply alternative news channels that wear the clothes of traditional sources but in fact promote nakedly partisan content. Shockateurs like Charlie Veitch or Paul Joseph Watson offer longer-form documentary content from 'extreme truth-tellers' designed to inform and 'amuse'. For some, these figures are trusted guides: one convert described Watson as 'very entertaining and quite truthful in his commentaries … about the state of the country' and of course, once watched, viewing spawns and serves up similar content through suggestions and reels.

At the more personalised end of the spectrum, influencer-led content on Instagram and TikTok delivers short, emotive bursts designed to provoke and mobilise, reinforced by the ease of sharing clips peer-to-peer. These platforms encourage an intimate, direct relationship between creator and viewer; they feel more 'private', less socially mediated. They provide a feeling of a one-on-one relationship with the influencer, and for younger users we found that these algorithmically curated feeds fast evolve into a closed-loop worldview. Instagram in particular very rapidly becomes a vector for extremist views: bite-sized content designed to provoke and enrage. It becomes clear that this social-media system is not, in fact, an echo-chamber. It is something far bigger; it is an entire ecosystem that creates, sustains, and above all normalises a particular worldview. To understand this, my fellow researchers and I realised we were going to have to study the eco-system itself.

To do this, I worked with ethical data-science company Signify to build a digital network map based on three UK X accounts – GB News, Reform UK and Matthew Goodwin. We chose these because polling indicates that they're go-to voices for voters leaning towards authoritarian-populist views. Between them they have more than 1.5 million followers on X, and from their public accounts Signify pulled a 30,000-follower sample, scraped who those people followed, and built a picture of the influencers shaping their world.

I was stunned by what emerged; it was not a British conversation at all – it was American. The top 20 most influential accounts were overwhelmingly US-based. At the centre? Elon Musk and Donald Trump, the dark suns with the gravitational mass to pull millions into their orbit. Seven of those 20 accounts Signify mapped are part of, or closely aligned with, the Trump political machine: Trump himself, his son, Vice President J.D. Vance, Robert F. Kennedy Jr. and the Department of Government Efficiency.

Only three of the top 20 are British (beyond GB News, Goodwin and Reform UK); Nigel Farage, Rupert Lowe and Tommy Robinson, the country's most notorious far-right agitator. Four of the US accounts push out hateful content at scale. End Wokeness, an anonymous account with 3.2 million followers, has amplified debunked claims about minorities; Bloomberg reported that Musk replied to it more than 420 times in two years. Alex Jones, who was previously found guilty of defaming Sandy Hook families, still pumps out white nationalist talking points. Libs of TikTok, with 4.3 million followers, is run by Chaya Raichik and pushes anti-LGBT content.

Even when Signify zoomed out to the top 200 accounts, the dominance was clear: nearly two-thirds of the accounts we mapped were American, just one-fifth British. Hungary, Canada, Ireland and Italy were also in the mix. Almost half were influencers – self-shot, direct-to-camera pundits blending politics with lifestyle branding. Some sell self-help or Bitcoin tips; others operate in the manosphere, channelling grievance into misogyny. Common threads are anti-trans rhetoric, climate denial and pandemic conspiracies. Some of the big names would not surprise you; Joe Rogan, the US podcast king, followed by Robinson, Kirk, End Wokeness, and Libs of TikTok. Monetisation is a constant subtext. Most offer paid subscriptions or solicit tips. Some promise to teach followers how to make 'tens of thousands' from X itself.

A quarter of the top 200 are politicians or officials – but four in five of them are American: Trump, Vance, Ron DeSantis, Ted Cruz, plus lesser-known hardliners like Jim Jordan and Byron Donalds. British names include Farage, Kemi Badenoch, Richard Tice, Lee Anderson, Boris Johnson – and Labour's Keir Starmer.

Just under 7 per cent are media outlets. GB News, Fox News and TalkTV are the only established broadcasters. The rest are hyper-partisan startups like the Daily Wire, Breitbart and Newsmax. Some 'news' accounts – Update NEWS, Wide Awake Media – have no masthead, no reporters, no physical footprint. Their posts are pure hit-and-run propaganda: inflammatory one-liners, video clips stripped of context, opinion dressed as fact. And Musk? The most influential node of all, he is openly contemptuous of 'legacy media' and happy to boost some of the most extreme voices in his online world.

If you take a step back and survey this scene, an extraordinary landscape comes into view. What has been built is a populist digital ecosystem tuned to a frequency of permanent outrage. But the irony is that Britain's populist right, forever shouting about sovereignty, is just another node in an American network. It is an extraordinary world. And, it turns out, it is a world that cost a good deal of cash to put together. And so, as with all things in politics, to really understand what is going on we have to follow the money.

7

Follow the Money

Mark Hanna, one-time US senator and campaign manager to President McKinley, once joked that there are only two things that matter in politics: the first is money – and he couldn't remember the second. The truth has not changed. Elections are expensive. Winners are not always the most persuasive; they are the best-financed. And what was true in the 1890s is true today. Mark Hanna's axiom endures: in politics, money matters. What differs is the way it moves. They key to understanding why populists are winning today is to grasp a singular truth – private fortunes now finance a populist media-political complex in which money buys distribution, distribution buys attention, and attention can be converted back into money – and votes.

Populism is a disruption and the populist business model is as radically disruptive as a Silicon Valley startup. Like all revolutions, it starts with a small band of believers. Only, these believers are not just fuelled by faith. They are armed with fortunes.

The rich and powerful have a long and well-documented fascination with power. In my study of Britain's long history of entrepreneurial brilliance,[1] I could not help but notice how many made their fortunes through a close proximity to the powerful people writing the rules of the game. I once asked Robert Watts, the editor of the *Sunday Times* Rich List about why he thought this happened. 'I think it's a combination of different things with different people,' Robert observed. 'With some, it's just, "Why can't these people get it right? Why can't they understand that we're the good guys ... we create finance for public services. So why don't they make it easier for us to do business?"' However, for others, as Robert explains, engaging in politics is a vanity trip: 'it is simply about power.'

To expose just how much money is facilitating Britain's populist surge, I worked with a brilliant young researcher, Adam Bychawski, to prepare a warning for the House of Commons Joint Committee on National Security Strategy. My aim was simple: to show how today's politics of disruption is bankrolled by a small group of people, building not merely a political party or supporting a handful of politicians but creating a new media-political complex designed to sustain the populist cause.

The market for political finance in Britain has long been susceptible to abuse. The rules reward secrecy, enable corruption and invite foreign interference. Foreign governments and hostile actors can pour cash into British politics through UK subsidiaries with few effective barriers to stop offshore assets being transferred onto our shores. Unincorporated associations are a second gaping hole through which bad actors can funnel millions without declaring sources; a UK company owned by a Swiss-German billionaire linked to funding Germany's far-right AfD was recently revealed to have channelled £250,000 to the Carlton Club, a regular donor to the Conservative

Party. So-called non-party campaigners can spend up to £10,000 on political ads without declaring a penny. In 2019, two such groups spent over £700,000 on anti-Labour adverts without declaring a single source.

Now, Reform-linked outfits such as the Great British PAC and Resolute 1850 are preparing to exploit the same loopholes. And with spending outside official election periods largely unregulated, and the Electoral Commission bereft of the enforcement powers it says it needs, the system is not merely porous, it is wide open.[2] Transparency International discovered that one pound in every ten donated to British parties came from 'unknown or questionable sources',[3] and while in 2024, RUSI told the House of Commons there are 'well-identified loopholes that allow for the possibility of donations from overseas sources',[4] those loopholes are now so enticing that one senior National Crime Agency official was blunt with me: 'the current political donation system contains vulnerabilities that are actively being exploited.'

To inform my work on the National Security Strategy, I asked my team to track all money flows from 1 January 2020 to 7 April 2025 – which involved scouring Electoral Commission returns, MPs' registers of interest, Companies House records, media reporting and US nonprofit filings. The result was jaw-dropping. We discovered £153 million sloshing through what has emerged as a populist media-political complex. And what it revealed was stark: never has so much political capacity been underwritten by so few private fortunes. Just three men – Paul Marshall, Christopher Chandler and Jeremy Hosking – or companies connected to these men, provide nine-tenths of the money. Just three men. Widen the lens to 2019, and a fourth man, Christopher Harborne, joins the cast. And here is a curiosity. Not only are two based overseas – Chandler in Dubai and Harborne in Thailand – but all made their fortunes in hedge funds or high finance.

Musing on this with a Conservative friend in the Commons coffee queue one morning, my colleague laughed when I shared the thought. 'That's not a coincidence,' he said. 'They've got one big thing in common with the people they fund. They all thrive on volatility.' And of course, he was right. In financial markets, a 'straddle' means buying both a call and a put option, so the trader profits whichever way the price moves – provided it moves far enough. The bet is not on direction but on disruption. Populist politics works in much the same way. For populists, stability is sterile, turbulence is fertile. Outrage, scandal, even defeat can be profitable. Each spike in volatility drives attention – and attention can be cashed. Through subscriptions, books, speaking tours, merchandise or even cryptocurrency schemes, the churn of public life becomes a revenue stream. Today's populists are not unlike volatility traders in the markets: they thrive on the swings, monetising outrage and converting chaos into cash.

So who are these characters?

First among equals is Paul Marshall – hedge-fund titan, philanthropist, one-time SDP activist, and now worth an estimated £875 million, earned at the helm of his hedge fund Marshall Wace, which now manages some £55 billion of assets.[5] In recent years, he has soured on the very liberal democracy in which he made his fortunes. 'Liberalism has lost its moorings,' he wrote in 2021, lamenting that the creed of progress had 'been pushed into every walk of life, defying any biblical understanding of human life'.[6]

Marshall has now poured hundreds of millions into academies, universities, churches and politics, and – according to our research – £55 million into media and political projects alone. It has not been plain sailing. In April 2024, he was forced to stand down from the chain of schools he founded after HOPE not hate exposed that his locked X account had reposted homophobic and Islamophobic content.[7]

Next comes Christopher Chandler, a New Zealand-born billionaire now based in Dubai. Chandler made his fortune during Russia's chaotic privatisation era, before founding the investment firm Legatum. From companies and organisations associated with Chandler we tracked some £77 million flowing into Britain's media-political complex, overwhelmingly to GB News, but with significant sums to the Association of Responsible Citizenship and the think tank Prosperity Institute. Quite how much was Chandler's personal wealth and how much came via Legatum is impossible to know because of course the UAE, where his firm is registered, is the world's eighth-most secretive tax jurisdiction, with almost no corporate transparency.

Jeremy Hosking is our third man; another financier turned mega-donor. Once a long-standing Conservative backer, Hosking – who amassed his fortune managing money – broke with the Tories to bankroll Laurence Fox's Reclaim Party, which accounts for a large slice of the £8 million worth of cheques we tracked.

Finally, we have Christopher Harborne, the Thai-based aviation entrepreneur with a major stake in British defence firm QinetiQ. His giving slowed after 2020 (a private office for Boris Johnson here, a private jet flight for Mr Farage there), but in 2019 he made his impact as one of Britain's single largest political donors, handing Reform UK £10 million in one year alone as part of a six-year £13 million spending spree. He then upped his stake in December 2025 by making the single largest donation by a living person to a British political party with a cheque for £9 million to Reform UK. Taken together, these four men form the financial backbone of Britain's populist media-political complex – fortunes made in hedge funds, finance and speculation now underwrite a politics that just so happens to thrive on volatility.

These are vast sums. But where are they going? 'Follow the money' is the oldest rule in political journalism – and when we traced the £153 million flowing into Britain's populist media-political complex, we were struck by a simple truth. Populist funders are not simply bankrolling parties. They are heeding the advice of Alain de Benoist, Pat Buchanan and Andrew Breitbart – that politics is downstream of culture – and so they are investing in the media end of the complex, bankrolling the 'polytainment' platforms that reward populist politicians with the currency of our age: attention, amplification, clicks and cash.

The single biggest bets are GB News (described as the 'pulpit of right-wing politics in Britain' by the *Financial Times*),[8] the opinion site UnHerd and culture-war magazine *The Critic*. Together, these three platforms absorbed more than £136 million from the four big donors in the four years we studied.

To understand what was happening here, I turned to Peter Geoghegan, the brilliant investigative journalist whose Substack, Democracy for Sale, has become essential reading for anyone who cares about the integrity of British politics.

'I think a lot of people misunderstand the media plays for Marshall,' Peter explained. 'They see it purely in terms of business, but that is to misread things. Marshall is a wealthy individual, and crucially, he was willing to start stumping up more money for GB News when it started losing money. That's when he transformed the scale of his investment to some £47 million.' But why? I asked.

'Because he sees in media an opportunity to influence politics. His strategy is, quite simply, to influence politics through the media and other para-political investments. He's less interested in who exactly is in power, and he is much more interested in whether his ideas and his ideology are the dominant ones. It's less about spending money for access. That's not what his play is. Rather, he's fighting a culture war. He wants to push the Overton window in Britain to the populist right in quite a dramatic way.' I don't know whether Mr Marshall has read Gramsci, but I do know that Gramsci would instantly recognise a 'war of position' when he saw it. But as our money hunt continued, a second truth emerged into sight: what you might call the trickle-down economics of populist media.

GB News not only offers a platform for British populists, it offers plenty of pound notes too: in total between 1 January 2020 and 7 April 2025, Reform's five MPs banked more than £1 million in earnings, gifts and donations; almost 40 per cent of that cash came from GB News; Nigel Farage took £295,737 as news host and his colleagues bagged another £100,000. And this no doubt helped leverage attention to social-media platforms, which generated another £40,000 for Reform's MPs from X alone. In just seven months.

But there is one final building block in the populists' new media-political complex: an effort not simply to cash in on the attention economy but to capitalise the earnings.

Mr Farage has created two companies: Farage Media Limited and Thorn in the Side Limited, which owns half a million shares in – you guessed it – GB News and which reported a £1.4 million cash surge in 2024.⁹

So there you have it; the new populist media-political complex. Funded by fortunes made offshore, obscured by corporate veils, titivated by think tanks that refuse to disclose their sponsors, and broadcast by platforms that have become both cheerleaders and paymasters. It has scaled rapidly since 2019. And if we want to know where this may all end up, we need look no further than President Trump's industrial-scale funding machine: a model that turns outrage into organisation, attention into assets and populism into profit.

The American hustle

Like Reform UK, President Trump's political machine owes a great deal to the fortunes of very few. Thanks to the US Supreme Court's *Citizens United* ruling in 2010 – described by Justice Ruth Bader Ginsburg as the worst decision of her tenure – there are now effectively no limits on political spending by corporations and outside groups. Any restraint is judged an infringement of the First Amendment, on the basis that companies possess the same free-speech rights as individuals. The result has been a flood tide of cash, mobilised by America's wealthiest through super PACs, which are now able to spend without limit so long as they maintain a paper-thin independence from formal campaigns.

Not long ago I had the chance to talk this over with Senator Bernie Sanders. 'If I were running for office,' explains Bernie, 'it would be totally legal for some group of billionaires to spend tens and tens of millions of dollars, hundreds of millions of dollars, against me, running TV ads, brochures and whatever they choose to do.' The so-called 'super PACs' – political action committees that draw donations together – will spend more money on a campaign than the candidate. 'So what does that do to politics?' I asked. He was blunt: 'the candidates become puppets to the puppeteer,' he replied.

I am sure that President Trump is no one's marionette. But nevertheless, the top ten donors to the President's re-election must surely be important. Together they stumped up almost half a billion dollars in super-PAC funding for the President – 44 per cent of his entire war-chest. However, as in Britain, this is only half the story, for what gave the President his real edge was the backing of a novel fusion of media platforms and political cash. President Trump's model went beyond cashing in on attention: he capitalised it, turning clicks into cash flows, cash flows into companies, and companies into stock, bought and sold on the stock exchange. This was not just campaign finance. It was the financialisation of attention itself.

When Donald Trump was evicted from Twitter and Facebook after the invasion of Congress on 6 January 2021, he did not just rage against the 'deep state' – he built his own megaphone and sold it. Truth Social, a Twitter clone, was launched in February 2022 as the flagship of Trump Media & Technology Group (TMTG). By early 2025 the site was claiming over 6 million active users – modest by the standards of Twitter or Facebook, but still a formidable echo-chamber, amplifying every attack line, grievance and conspiracy. But its real genius lay in the way it was monetised. To go public the company cut a deal with a Special Purpose Acquisition Company (SPAC), a shell firm created with no business of its own, just a pot of cash and a promise to merge with a future target.

In March 2024, Trump's TMTG merged with Digital World Acquisition Corp and, overnight, Truth Social was valued in the billions. President Trump's personal 60 per cent stake was suddenly worth, on paper at least, $4–6 billion. Initially locked-out from selling his shares, the President still found ways to pledge them as collateral for loans. It was a masterclass in financial alchemy: turning political anger into speculative gold. Outrage was not just weaponised – it was securitised, floated, and traded like a brand of bottled anger. But the echo-chamber was about to get bigger.

From the moment Elon Musk took over Twitter in October 2022, he became the platform's amplifier-in-chief. Platform changes increased the visibility of Musk's messages – including his support for Trump – and the reach was extraordinary. But Musk went further, investing $277 million through two super PACs to run ads, hire staff, and at one point even pioneer a $1 million daily giveaway to registered swing-state voters.[10]

When the President crossed the winning line from opposition into government, his critics would argue that he took one unfortunate step forward.

When I first began studying the political economy of corruption, I turned to my old friend James Crabtree, the former *Financial Times* correspondent in India and author of *The Billionaire Raj*. James explained to me how the most sophisticated players in India made sure they maximised their upside from power: *they take equity*. And that is undeniably what is happening now in America but with a digital twist and on a staggering new scale.

As Eric Trump was soon to realise, the lustre and levers of the presidency were very, very valuable: 'We're the hottest brand in the world right now,'[11] he declared. Money has poured in from media sources. CBS's *60 Minutes* settled a dispute with $16 million on the table. ABC resolved a lawsuit with $15 million soon after. Jeff Bezos has promised Melania Trump a fortune for her exclusive story for Amazon Prime. Truth Social, despite its weakness as a business, has added $25 million to the family balance sheet. Licensing deals have been sealed to plaster the Trump brand on perfumes, sneakers and mobile phones. Mar-a-Lago alone has generated an additional $125 million; the Trump's Washington hotel now fills with lobbyists and foreign dignitaries, and the Trump family has opened an expensive new Washington club called Executive Branch.

Around the world, the family business has boomed. In *Autocracy, Inc.*, Pulitzer Prize-winning journalist Anne Applebaum describes the constellation of strongmen autocrats around the world as devoted not to ideology but to self-enrichment and as cementing their bonds with each other 'not through ideals, but through deals'.[12] Since the President returned to office, his family deal-flow has been non-stop; Trump's organisation has struck deals across the Gulf, planned a Trump Tower in Saudi Arabia, a hotel in Amman, a golf club in Vietnam, and luxury property schemes in India, Serbia and Albania. The Qatari royal family has even gone to the length of proposing to gift it a $400 million private jet, glittering in what has been described as 'regional car dealership Rococo'.[13]

But nothing is as valuable as a currency of your own to sell. The President used to be highly sceptical of cryptocurrency, dismissing the idea as 'a disaster waiting to happen' and 'like the drug trade'. But it is very popular around Mr Trump's billionaire backers and indeed in spaces like the manosphere.

In his investigations, James Bloodworth was surprised at just how often crypto-promotion appeared. As he put it, the attraction was 'like that hidden knowledge of this kind of secretive currency that's outside of mainstream institutions'. Many of the men drawn into these spaces, James explained, 'are not university-educated or college-educated … they're not necessarily financially successful, and then something like crypto is presented to them as a get-rich-quick scheme by a lot of these manosphere self-help right-wing figures online'. The pitch is always the same: the mainstream are 'just conformists', but if you 'learn the secrets of cryptocurrency, you're going to be richer than all of those people'. That promise, wrapped in the imagery of 'mansions and Lamborghinis and stuff (all hired)', is really just another hustle: 'buy my course on crypto, you can get rich like me … but the reason they have money is from selling courses, not from any business.'

I doubt it was the manosphere's influence but, by 2024, President Trump had had an epiphany. Before he re-entered the White House, the President opened a new business with property developer Steve Witkoff, called World Liberty Financial, which proceeded to roll out a suite of branded tokens – the $TRUMP meme coin, a Melania coin, and a governance token, WLFI. These crypto coins are not investments in any normal sense. They are more like cigarette cards for the digital age: branded collectibles, the only value for which comes from the hype of ownership and the hope that someone else will pay more for them tomorrow. But each time they are bought, sold or traded, a slice of the transaction (75 per cent of the money raised from token sales)[14] flows back to Trump-linked entities. The 'investor' gets nothing in return – no share of profits, no ownership rights, no claim on assets. It is grievance financialised: sold back to those who feel they have the least. Supporters were not buying shares in a company. They were speculative chips in a casino with rules written by the house. And the house was the Trump family. Whether the tokens soared or collapsed, the family still won. Which did nothing to deter buyers like Justin Sun, who won a $100,000 watch for investing $20 million in meme coins around the time the US Securities and Exchange Commission (SEC) dropped its civil fraud cases against him.

This little side-hustle has proved to have geopolitical muscle. From flogging meme coins to true believers, WLFI soon began offering dollar-pegged stablecoin credible enough for Abu Dhabi Investment Authority to stump up a $2 billion investment, while a Chinese-linked tech firm lined up $300 million to scoop up $TRUMP tokens. Populism once financialised has now been internationalised. By mid-2025, the President's own financial disclosure confirmed $57.4 million in personal earnings from World Liberty,[15] and *Forbes* estimates Trump made $1 billion in just nine months, with crypto now accounting for up to 80 per cent of his net worth. *The New Yorker* estimates crypto ventures have made $2.37 billion for the Trump family.[16] By coincidence, the Justice Department has begun dropping probes into illegal crypto-use. IRS prosecutions have been discouraged. SEC rules have been loosened.

All told, at the time of writing, *The New Yorker*'s comprehensive survey estimates that the President's family has now amassed an estimated $3.4 billion through ventures spanning hospitality, Gulf investments, crypto schemes, NFTs and Truth Social.[17] The scale of this money-making, Anne Applebaum assured me, may not be unknown in autocracies around the world – but it is unprecedented in a modern democracy with a dangerous new mechanism: creating pseudo-commercial vehicles – especially crypto tokens – that give supporters no real asset or rights, but function as open channels to transfer money to the President's family. And this, Anne warns, may become a new playbook for kleptocracy that others will copy, because it industrialises what used to be covert quid-pro-quo into routinised 'business', narrowing the air gap between democratic and autocratic practice. The risk, Anne concludes, is not merely personal enrichment but a system in which governance is continuously arbitraged for cash – and emulated abroad.

The significance of this is not just the money. It is the way scandal fuels loyalty rather than questions it. For critics, these revelations are proof of corruption: a presidency turned into a family business. For supporters, Trump's enrichment demonstrates strength and cunning. Transparency International warned that President Trump is treating public office 'as if he owned it', more monarch than President. Yet for millions of followers, this is precisely the point. His power to bend global finance, Gulf monarchs and even the US regulatory state to his advantage proves his dominance. This is the populist paradox: every scandal deepens the myth.

It will amaze you to learn that Reform UK are as keen on cryptocurrency as President Trump himself. The party has announced it will take donations in bitcoin.[18] In the UK, mega-donor Christopher Harborne was reported to have received $70 million in Tether tokens in 2019, shortly before donating around £13 million to the Brexit Party and other causes.[19] Another £9 million had been donated at the time of writing. George Cottrell, an aide to Nigel Farage, has been accused of laundering cryptocurrency to fund a political party, from his base in in Montenegro (allegations he has strenuously denied).[20] Announcing plans in Las Vegas of all places, Mr Farage said Reform UK would transform Britain with a 'crypto revolution' by slashing capital-gains tax on crypto assets, allowing people to pay their taxes in cryptocurrency, and even establish a national 'Bitcoin reserve fund'. Yet here is the risk: not only do these techniques leave our democracies wide open to infiltration by bad actors; they leave our politics open to bad states, in particular the Russian state, which is on the hunt for new vectors of influence.

The darkest money

Russian military doctrine has always reserved a special place for *active measures* – a strategy first pioneered in the 1920s, designed to sow discord and division without firing a shot. In the mid-2010s, a new toolkit emerged, often mislabelled the Gerasimov doctrine, after the then chief of Russia's armed forces. It blended conventional force with information warfare, political subversion, cyber attacks, economic coercion and covert action. The aim was clear: fracture Western unity, weaken democratic institutions, and exploit any social faultlines in sight.

The logic is straightforward. Democracies thrive on differences of opinion. Push those differences to extremes, and you paralyse the system. Elections became the point of maximum opportunity, and social media – tuned as it is to turn the mildest disagreement into a raging row – became the perfect weapon. A former NATO Supreme Commander in Europe once described the philosophy to me like this: 'Russia's goal is to fracture political cohesion across Europe – and far-right parties are effective tools to do just that.'

Russian interference in Western politics is now documented fact. In 2020, Parliament's Intelligence and Security Committee was blunt: 'The UK is clearly a target for Russia's disinformation campaigns and political influence operations ... the government has badly underestimated the response needed.'[21] Across the Atlantic, the US Senate Committee on Foreign Relations found the Kremlin had been cultivating ties with US alt-right networks to stoke political divisions and amplify Russia-friendly narratives.[22] It concluded: 'many extreme right-wing groups, including white nationalists, look up to Putin'.

The methods are varied, but the playbook is consistent. Loans from Kremlin-linked banks; covert shell companies; political partnerships like Austria's Freedom Party alliance with United Russia; propaganda pumped through RT and Sputnik; bot-driven disinformation; and a web of NGOs and think tanks laundering the Kremlin line.[23] And the sums are big. Since 2014, US intelligence has assessed that Russia has covertly transferred over $300 million to political parties, officials and politicians across more than two dozen countries.[24] That is a lot of Russian rubles for Russia's poodles, and populist parties appeared to be first in line with their bank books.

In France, Marine Le Pen's National Rally took a €9.4 million loan from the First Czech-Russian Bank in 2014 – arranged, as investigations by Mediapart and the *Washington Post* showed, to evade EU oversight. She has openly praised Putin as a 'patriot' who 'defends the interests of his country'.[25] In Italy, BuzzFeed News published leaked tapes of Kremlin operatives discussing funnelling oil profits to Matteo Salvini's right-wing Lega party, and Salvini himself wore Putin T-shirts in Moscow, calling him 'the best statesman currently on Earth'.[26] Austria's Freedom Party not only signed a cooperation pact with Putin's United Russia party but imploded in 2019 when its leader was filmed offering contracts to a supposed oligarch's niece in the notorious 'Ibiza' scandal. Germany's AfD has echoed Russian narratives on Crimea and sanctions, with members appearing regularly on Russia Today and Sputnik. In 2024, *Der Spiegel* alleged Russia-backed media portal Voice of Europe was flowing cash to European politicians with right-wing extremist parties, including the AfD's Maximilian Krah and Petr Bystron.[27] Hungary's Viktor Orbán has gone further: praising Putin's 'illiberal democracy' and using Hungary's EU veto to shield Moscow's interests. Meanwhile in the UK, the former Welsh leader of Reform UK Nathan Gill was jailed in 2025 for accepting money while he served as an MEP – money from a man described by the US government as a 'pawn' of Russian secret services and acting on behalf of a 'close friend' of Vladimir Putin. The pattern is unmistakable. Moscow nurtures Europe's far right not just with words but with money, media and manipulation – feeding a cycle of grievance that weakens the West from within.

Russian effectiveness, however, took a big hit in the wake of the global backlash that followed its use of nerve-agent attacks on the streets of an English market town, and its invasion of Ukraine. A combination of sanctions and huge deportation of intelligence officers severely dented Russian capabilities. But the Kremlin quickly adapted. Having tested crypto-based financing in the ransomware trade, the Russian Intelligence Service now uses cryptocurrency to fund overseas foreign-influence operations.

When someone buys a cryptocurrency, the transaction itself is recorded on the blockchain and is publicly visible – but their identity is anonymous. So far we know that this anonymity has allowed cryptocurrencies to be used to fund everything from sanctions evasion to election interference. The Centre for Information Resilience recently revealed that A7A5,[28] a new 'digital ruble', has already been linked to sanctions evasions by Russians. The report also found that Ilan Shor, a fugitive oligarch who has been accused of being involved with Russian-backed attempts to meddle in Moldovan elections, had allegedly used the currency to funnel at least $39m (£29 million) into the bank accounts of thousands of Moldovans in exchange for their votes.

This is the new frontier of campaign financing. Cryptocurrencies give people plenty of ways to hide, obscuring who is funding political parties and what they might want in return. Online 'mixers' can blend an individual's cryptocurrency with others, making it practically impossible to trace the origin of individual coins.

People can also donate using multiple crypto wallets with different addresses, splitting large donations into smaller amounts that bypass the reporting thresholds for political donations. This is a system that risks borderless currencies sidestepping money-laundering checks through decentralised platforms that operate in a grey zone beyond the law. They are almost custom-built for hostile actors, and wide open to abuse, especially by those who launder foreign money into the bank accounts of UK citizens before passing it on to British political parties.

Yet there is one more source of funding that we cannot ignore. Indeed, Russia's gifts may now pale into insignificance compared to the largesse of the American Christian right.

Faith-based funding has, in recent years, become a critical source of funding for populist politics in Britain. Paul Marshall – the GB News investor – is a devout evangelical Christian, worshipping at the well-funded Holy Trinity Brompton, to which he has donated some £5 million, alongside £10 million to the Church Revitalisation Trust. As Peter Geoghegan told me, faith may indeed be Marshall's principal motivation. In France too, faith is the principal motivation inspiring Pierre-Edouard Stérin, a billionaire caught on video leaning quite close to the tropes of the *Grand Remplacement*,[29] who says he plans to spend €80 million a year funding Catholic good-causes charities, associations and heritage projects along with €150 million to political causes including Marine Le Pen's Rassemblement National.

But faith networks are bigger than any one individual. Between 2019 and 2023, one authoritative study found that these groups funnel more than $20 million a year into Europe, sustaining a vast ecosystem of litigation shops, think tanks, broadcasters, and campaigners worth well over a billion dollars. At its centre sit the litigators – Alliance Defending Freedom International and the European Centre for Law and Justice – taking case after case to the courts. Alongside them, the World Youth Alliance trains new cadres for the politics of grievance. The Christian Broadcasting Network saturates airwaves, pouring over $60 million into Europe in just five years. To this effort must be added the work of the Leadership Institute, the Cato Institute, and Family Watch International, which export US-born campaigns against 'gender ideology' into European legislatures.

And where does this cash land? In the coffers of Spain's Vox, fuelling Margarita de la Pisa Carrión's relentless assault on reproductive rights. In Poland, where NGOs linked to the Law and Justice Party thrive on American dollars. In France, where Rassemblement National and Reconquête! are buoyed by Catholic allies. In Hungary, where Viktor Orbán's Fidesz has fused Christian nationalism with authoritarianism, making Budapest the capital of Euro-MAGA. And now in Brussels, where the Patriots for Europe bloc bids to reshape the European Parliament from within. Supporting this work is a transatlantic connection which is very well oiled, thanks to organisations like the Alliance for Responsible Citizenship (ARC). Founded by US populist podcaster Jordan Peterson, its second global conference in London in 2025 boasted a guest list stretching from Peter Thiel to Douglas Murray to Nigel Farage. Marshall and Peterson are closely connected: in 2022 Marshall's Sequoia Trust gave £18 million to Ralston College, whose chancellor is Peterson himself.

Although these funders present as charity, the money is in fact strategy. It may involve compassion, but it is most definitely about control. Not merely philanthropy but politics. Money is being shifted from pulpits in Colorado Springs into the war-chests of Europe's populists. Its purpose is clear: to ensure that the culture wars so familiar to Americans cross the Atlantic and turn sermons into statutes.

One hundred and thirty years after Mark Hanna quipped that politics could be understood only by following the money, the lesson still holds true. From clicks to crypto to Christianity, populists have built a formidable machine: raising vast sums of money, converting money into votes, and votes into power. It is an extraordinary operation – but it can be stopped.

Conclusion

How to Beat Them

A little after 1 p.m. on the afternoon of Saturday 4 March 1933, the 51-year-old Franklin Roosevelt, paralysed from the waist down, braced himself on the arm of his son and climbed the marble steps to the wooden rostrum beneath the massive Corinthian columns and sculpted pediment of the US Capitol's East Front. Above him the Washington skies were cold and grey. Before him stood the radio microphones, ready – for the first time in history – to take an inauguration speech to the world. Beyond them, 150,000 assembled Americans stood in silence, hollow-eyed from years of bank failures and breadlines. Over the next 15 minutes, Roosevelt delivered the most important speech in American history after Lincoln's Gettysburg Address. And in just over eighteen hundred words, he tabled the formula required to defeat populism today.

In a clear, confident, almost defiant voice, Roosevelt declared, 'The only thing we have to fear is fear itself,' as he set out a plan to turn that fear into faith, paralysis into purpose, and despair into action. 'Restoration calls ... not for changes in ethics alone,' he explained, '[t]his Nation asks for action, and action now.' Roosevelt's creed was simple: put people to work, confront corruption, and bend government not just to act, but to deliver for the common good.

The same muscular courage is needed now. When faith falters and fear rises, populists prey on despair. They tell people the game is rigged and that only a strong man can fix it. They build movements bound more by grievance than by hope, financed by dark money and fuelled by digital rage.

Populism is what rebellion looks like in a democracy. But the answer cannot be outrage alone. Defeating populism requires three things. First, mobilise a majority bigger than the populist bloc, by lifting living standards, restoring pride in place, and rebuilding trust that government can work. Second, take apart their story and beat them on their own terrain – exposing their economic fantasies, their selective patriotism, and their falsehoods on social media. Third, shut off the dark money that finances their bleak ambitions, along with the shell companies, offshore havens, and crypto cash that link populism to kleptocracy.

Over the last year, through hundreds of interviews, focus groups and research across Britain and beyond, a clear ten-point plan has emerged – a Rooseveltian strategy of renewal for the age of AI and algorithmic anger. It is a plan to reunite the centre ground, out-communicate the extremes and out-perform those who root their appeal in division. This is how we turn despair into determination and prove once again that democracy can deliver, just as Franklin Roosevelt delivered almost a century ago.

1. The heroic coalition

Out on the campaign trail, the American statesman Adlai Stevenson was once greeted by a gushing supporter. 'Every thinking person in America', she enthused 'will be voting for you.' 'I'm afraid that won't do,' Stevenson shot back. 'I need to win a majority.'

In democracies, majorities are the foundation of power. Good political strategy begins with clarity about the coalition of voters required to beat the opposition. All good political leaders must know: 'who are we for?' But that basic discipline often goes missing in action. The veteran political strategist Alistair Campbell summed it up for me: 'right now, I see a lot of politics. What I don't see is a lot of political strategy.'

In the UK, at the last election in 2024, the Labour Party had that clarity. Based on the work of Dame Deborah Mattinson, Labour sought to win what Deborah called 'the hero voter'; 'typically non-college educated parents who work full time, have an average age of 42 – are disillusioned with politics and under constant financial pressure'.[1]

But to defeat populism today, mainstream politics needs more than a heroic voter: it needs a heroic coalition. What magic, I asked Patrick English, head of politics at YouGov, is required to conquer extremism? 'It's coalition-building, isn't it?' He replied, 'It's "base plus". It's [knowing] who are your base and what can you stick on to move you from 20 per cent [of voters] to 30–35 per cent.'

Professor Jane Green and her colleagues have explained the psephology.[2] The shockwaves that have hit Britain over the last 20 years have shaken voters across the spectrum like points of light in a kaleidoscope. What has emerged is an electorate that is crystallising into two new divisions, but within each division party affinities are scattered. 'The Brexit realignment hasn't disappeared,' explained Professor Green, 'it has hardened into two blocs.' On one side stands the left-liberal Remain bloc – Labour, the Lib Dems, the Greens, the SNP. On the other, the right-conservative Leave bloc – the Conservatives and Reform UK.

The risk for the left is the fragility of its bloc, the 'progressive coalition'; the 2024 alliance of tactical and liberal voters may not automatically re-form at the next election. It has to be remobilised because, as I write, it is splintering between Greens, Lib Dems, Independents – and apathy. If faced with a united right bloc, in which Reform prevails, Labour faces peril in over 80 seats where Reform already runs second or a close third. Bottom line? Progressives must keep the right divided, reunite the left-liberal coalition and flip at least some of the two most persuadable tribes of Reform-minded voters.

My work with Best for Britain and YouGov shows this is possible. As we've seen, Reform's supporters are not a single army marching in step but a fragile alliance of five 'tribes' bound more by discontent than common convictions. So progressives shouldn't base their strategy on aiming to persuade the unpersuadable, the most extreme of populist supporters. Rather, progressives should couple a strategy of uniting left-bloc voters with two of the 'tribes of Reform' – up to 40 per cent of Farage's base.

These folk worry about pay, pensions, bills, social security and the NHS. They are open to Labour, the Lib Dems, even the Greens. But how are they best detached from Reform? Our work showed a 'Premier League' of messages and ideas works best.

First: the economy. Nigel Farage has tabled billions of pounds' worth of unfunded promises. That means higher mortgages, higher bills, higher prices. Second: employment rights. Reform would scrap safeguards on sick pay, safe hours and zero-hours contracts. Third: social security, where Reform-considerers worry that Reform might axe support for pensioners, families and disabled people, leaving the vulnerable out in the cold. Fourth: the NHS. Reform has mused openly about a US-style insurance model, threatening free provision at the point of need.

These beliefs alarm a lot of Reform's would-be supporters. By contrast, attacks painting Reform's leader as 'Britain's Trump' or focusing on immigration move the dial less. Populists thrive when debate rages on their chosen turf of immigration and identity. We have to fix our immigration system – but let us not pitch our biggest fights on their battlefield.

As we set about this task, there is one further imperative for rebuilding the 'decent majority'. Populism, as Peter Hyman reminded me, is less an argument than a feeling. It's an emotional revolt, not an ideological one. It's the cry of people who feel looked down upon by a class that stopped listening. Too often, progressives dismiss that anger as grievance politics. But, as Hyman puts it to me, 'Every time someone on the left says that, what it means is, I don't think it's real.' What the left calls grievance, he insists, is often justified pain. 'It's not grievance if you've not had a pay rise for fifteen years.'

The antidote, argues Peter, is not another comms grid or sharper messaging, but a change of mindset – genuine curiosity about people's lives. 'I think it's 70 per cent of all of this,' he says. 'It's sort of deep listening that is a day by day by day thing.' Unless politics once again becomes an act of listening – not just transaction but relationship – then new policies will rest on sand. Until progressives show they truly get the texture of people's days – their hopes, their humiliations, their hunger for respect – no policy offer, however generous, will cut through. Only then can we turn justified anger into common purpose and rebuild faith in a politics that earns back the people's trust and lays the groundwork for rekindling the rocket-fuel of progressive politics: optimism.

2. Progressive optimism

Oscar Wilde once defined a pessimist as 'one who, when he has the choice of two evils, chooses both'. Which is why pessimists make bad electoral choices. Doom and decline form the double helix of populists' DNA. From President Trump to Nigel Farage to Viktor Orbán, the motif is always the same – our country is broken, our civilisation is dying, we've lost who we are. As we read in Chapter 4, this 'dark specialism' has a long lineage back to the work of Oswald Spengler in the 'morbid age' of the 1920s.

This pessimism must be defeated because pessimism is ruinous for sensible reformers. It saps the energy required for difficult journeys. It risks, as John Maynard Keynes once explained, trapping us between 'two opposed errors ... the pessimism of the revolutionaries who think that things are so bad that nothing can save us but violent change, and the pessimism of the reactionaries who consider the balance of our economic and social life so precarious that we must risk no experiments'.[3]

Optimism, by contrast, is like wind in the sails. All kinds of new adventures become possible. I have long been fascinated by this. On the doorsteps of my constituency, I asked voters about this a lot during the last election. What I found is that people desperately want tomorrow to be better but they are wrestling with 'the three impossibles':

1. Isn't a new golden age impossible?
2. Isn't a share of progress for ordinary people impossible?
3. Isn't it impossible for you to deliver, when, to coin a phrase, there is no money – and we can't see the difference between you and the other parties?

Plausible optimism demands we answer all three questions and defeat the Jeremiahs who counsel that economic dynamism is impossible in an ageing society. We are not short of prophets of doom, like American economist Robert Gordon who argues that economic growth will only now stutter because after the great breakthroughs of the first three industrial revolutions – steam and railways, electricity and combustion engines, computers and the web – innovation is 'battering its head against the wall of diminishing returns'.[4]

I disagree. Technology is a consistent surprise. Change is now so fast that yesterday's science fiction is a daily reality: bionic limbs, mobile phones, artificial intelligence, 3D printing, tablets, space stations, driverless cars – once the stuff of *Metropolis*, *Star Trek*, *A Space Odyssey*, *The Fifth Element* or *I, Robot* – are already with us. And in the future, the combined power of artificial intelligence, quantum computing, global gigabit connectivity, genome sequencing, gene editing, the green transition and the ceaseless rise of the global middle class will transform our fortunes. Such is tomorrow's potential that the head of the International Monetary Fund, Kristalina Georgieva,[5] argues that over the course of the life of a baby born today, living standards could multiply by anywhere between three and thirteen fold.

Successful progressive parties – such John F Kennedy's Democratic Party and Harold Wilson's Labour Party – channel optimism. Kennedy electrified America with his vision of a 'new frontier'. Wilson set out a series of papers and speeches – 'Signposts for the Sixties', 'Labour and the Scientific Revolution' – before delivering a sizzling speech by the Scarborough seaside that argued Britain must embrace the 'white heat' of the technological revolution. Like Kennedy, this magic won him an election, not merely with an arresting phrase but a vision of the future, the consequential challenges, the plan to meet the challenges and a sense of how the abundant harvest of tomorrow would be fairly shared. And here the lesson of Keynes's famous essay – 'Economic Possibilities for our Grandchildren' – is an important warning.

Writing in 1930, Keynes forecast that, by 2030, the standard of life in 'progressive countries' would be four to eight times higher than in 1930. He was broadly right. In advanced economies, real income per person is roughly 7–10 times higher. But while living standards have risen and working hours shrunk, we are not enjoying the average 15-hour work week that Keynes foresaw because Keynes had not reckoned with spiralling inequality. The lesson for progressives today is simple. Embrace the future. But unless we explain just how it will be fairly shared, we will fail.

The founder of YouGov, Peter Kellner, is one of the best political thinkers I know. He distilled the lesson for me with typical acuity. 'The antidote', he explained, 'is basically optimism plus fairness.' Defeating populism requires two elements working together. Optimism provides the sense of hope that tomorrow can be better than today. Fairness assures us that hope is credible. And that is why optimism must be a clear plan for rebuilding what Gordon Brown used to call the opportunity economy.

3. *The opportunity economy*

The epidemic of discontent that has triggered modern populism has been caused by a double has been squeeze on capital; on the one hand, household capital has been squeezed by a multi-generational crunch on income and, on the other, the social capital that was once the glue that held communities – and nations – together has been transformed and reduced by modern life. Populist voters share a deep sense of economic disappointment, insecurity, unfairness and an impoverished community spirit. Many are in midlife, looking towards retirement not with hope but anxiety. To beat populism, we have to tackle the root causes of this anxiety.

Let's start with the economics. In the UK, half of the most hardline Reform supporters say they are worse off than they expected to be at this stage of life. A third expect their wealth to fall over the next decade. Two-thirds believe their children will be poorer than they are. Voters describe lives that have shifted from thriving to coping with rising bills, stagnant wages and the conviction that hard work no longer pays. Eight in ten of the most disillusioned Reform voters believe their local area is in serious decline, twice the national average. They see boarded-up shops, shuttered halls and fly-tipped streets as symbols of abandonment.

To add insult to injury, there is a deeply held belief that taxes (on them) are too high, that 'people like me don't get our fair share' and that most government spending is wasted. Populist-leaning voters feel they've paid in but get little back. In the UK, Reform's rise is built on resentment, neglect and the feeling of having done the right things, only to be left behind by a system that no longer seems to work for them. To stand any chance of creating an economic model that helps tackle this, progressives must move on from 'Bidenomics', the formula of the last Democratic President.

Bidenomics rejected 40 years of trickle-down economics and attempted to rebuild America's productive base and middle class through public investment, worker power, and industrial policy. It had a lot of the right ideas, but many progressives argued that it was over-friendly to corporate America. Republicans derided 'big government socialism'. Critics on both sides of the aisle warned its vast bills fuelled inflation, protectionism and subsidy wars with allies. And in 2024 it failed at the polls. As one Democratic economist put it to me, 'we thought the American voters would accept a trade of a hot labour market and a little inflation'. That was a miscalculation for America, and it is the wrong prescription for the future.

Long-term investment – especially in infrastructure – is important. But more important still is a 'New Deal for the Age of AI': real help now to ease the pressure on living standards, a bold new plan to diffuse technology through the base of small and medium-sized businesses that employ between half and two-thirds of workers across the West,[6] and serious investment into building what President Macron once called the Learning Society.

To understand what real help is needed, I worked with Best for Britain and YouGov to gather the best ideas of think tanks and experts and tested them with voters. The results were stark. Reform considerers are driven above all by a living-standards crisis, not ideology. Overwhelmingly, the priorities were reducing energy bills, raising the personal tax-free allowance and cutting income tax. Only small minorities prioritised traditional welfare measures such as council-tax support or social care.[7]

To sustain rising standards of living in the future, we have to deliver a pay rise for Britain. And that requires a more productive Britain. Yet since the global financial crisis, UK and European productivity has seriously lagged behind the United States.[8] The American worker now completes by mid-morning on a Thursday what it takes a British worker till the end of Friday to produce. So rather than bet everything on big, long-term infrastructure spending, the UK needs to learn a lesson from the dawn of the Industrial Revolution when, after the great breakthroughs of the Scientific Revolution, an age of diffusion dawned as new thinking suffused through the old medieval economy. Britain invented more because new thinking spread faster through novel networks like Birmingham's Lunar Society or London's Royal Society, and new institutions from the Royal Navy to the Bank of England. Knowledge was no longer a private preserve but the lifeblood of a new, connected age.

Today we need a similar revolution. We need the infrastructure of the next industrial era, like chips, grids and gigafactories. But more importantly, we need to democratise access to the technologies they enable. We need institutions and incentives that carry innovation from the frontier of science to the factory floor, offices and high streets. And that will require a transformation in the way we build a Learning Society.[9]

The old factory model of education – one teacher, one classroom, one curriculum – was built for a world of repetition. Now we live in an age of perpetual invention. What is needed today is a system where every citizen learns how to learn and every community becomes a school. That requires new institutions: digital campuses without walls, public learning labs where workers and citizens can experiment, university campuses in left-behind towns that connect colleges and higher education together to retrain, to re-equip and provide the space for new entrepreneurs young and old to make a start and scale up. Education must become a common good, as vital to democracy as clean air or safe streets – where everyone is empowered – as they are in countries like Singapore, with individual learnings accounts – just as we have pension savings accounts – as the best insurance in a world of change. That will not come free. But we can afford it, if we restore a hard-edged fairness to the way the country works.

4. Renew the 'fairness code'

A key reason that populists are winning is because millions now feel the 'fairness code'[10] that is the foundation of our communal life together is well and truly broken. People who have done everything right – worked hard, paid taxes, raised families – feel cheated by a system that no longer seems to reward their effort, and let down by politicians who are failing to fix it.

Many Reform voters live by a fierce ethic of self-reliance: 'I go to work every day to pay my way ... I don't expect handouts,' as one put it. Yet for all the hard graft, millions see themselves going backwards while others appear to get something for nothing. Our polling with Best for Britain revealed that most hardcore Reform voters overwhelmingly believe that 'life in today's Britain is a lottery: you have to be born in the right family or get lucky to succeed' and that 'The UK's economy is rigged to advantage the rich and powerful.' But this grievance fuses economics with identity and a belief that, not only is the system rigged for the rich above, it is tilted towards minorities or immigrants below. As one focus group reported, 'We've become second-class citizens in our own home.' Resentment rises whenever a moral code of reciprocity is seen to fail and when people feel 'I've had it hard – why should anyone else have it easy?'

Resentments like these become acute when people are convinced that the world has become a zero-sum game. The experience of multi-generational decline and a profound pessimism about the future is, as Ben Page put it to me, 'a massive psychological change' that brings with it a sense that 'suddenly we're into zero-sum economics ... that if other people are getting something, I'm not.' The morality of a fairness where we share gains surrenders to a defensive scramble to protect what little remains. As Page puts it, 'You can be more generous when you think everything's getting better.' But when it isn't, you can't. That is why populist messages about protection – keeping out migrants, defending 'our own' – resonate so strongly. They promise moral order in place of economic hope. When fear of the future replaces faith in progress, fairness itself is re-imagined as a zero-sum struggle.

Zero-sum thinking is lethal for those of us who believe in cooperative politics. So, to rekindle support for the collaborative ideal, we must renew the nation's fairness code.

Progressives care deeply about fairness. We put the notion in our thinking, philosophy and slogans. But as Jonathan Haidt once put it, 'Everyone cares about fairness but there are two major kinds. On the left, fairness often implies equality, but on the right it means proportionality – people should be rewarded in proportion to what they contribute, even if that guarantees unequal outcomes.'[11] A fairness code that convinces voters that the future will indeed be fairly shared requires both ideas. Tony Blair expressed the ideal well: 'A modern notion of citizenship gives rights but demands obligations, shows respect but wants it back, grants opportunity but insists on responsibility.'

In today's Britain, renewing the fairness code demands big moves on immigration, social security and tax, together with new antagonists for our storyline. Our answers cannot entail redistribution alone; they must honour work, effort and reciprocity,[12] and call out those who profit yet fail these tests.

We will not defeat populism for good without fixing our immigration system. That means fixing border security – and something more: the unfinished business from my time as immigration minister when I set out to redesign the newcomers' path to citizenship.

During my days in the Home Office, I spent months on the road, talking to thousands of people around the country about just what they expected of newcomers. It was a remarkable journey. What I heard was a nation that was then comfortable with difference, tolerant, firm in its belief in 'live and let live' but that expected newcomers to sign up to some basic rules of the road.

That is why, I argued, we need a clear route through probationary citizenship to check newcomers really have truly committed to a British life and to signal that citizenship is a privilege earned through contribution and conduct. Along the way, obligations should deepen. Stronger English language skills are essential – for integration, for mobility, for fairness. Those who break the law should be deported. And aside from refugees and marriage routes, newcomers should make a steady tax contribution for at least five years.

Along that path, we must arrange fairly the moment when rights and benefits are granted because today's patchwork of entitlements undermines confidence and blurs the link between rights and responsibilities. But the principle of earned citizenship offers a clearer, fairer story: one where commitment is rewarded, belonging is built, and the value of British citizenship is restored as a visible marker of contribution, responsibility and shared national life, which of course begins in the communities where we live.

Second, we have to restore the something-for-something deal at the heart of social security. Right now, millions of populist voters feel they pay in and get nothing else. That is why I argue for universal basic capital: a Universal Savings Account for everyone when they start work into which we save a bit automatically and into which goes a special one-off dividend for every young person, as a tax break or a savings match worth up to £10,000, to help them put down a deposit on a home to call their own. Think of it like a Premium Bond – paid out by the nation to the next generation. If it was paid into a Universal Savings Account as a savings match or tax break, it would be hugely popular.

That money would come from a new national sovereign wealth fund that would take time to build – but which could be built much faster by restoring fairness to the tax system. Right now, our tax code simply does not reflect our moral code. It is riddled with loopholes. At the time I wrote my previous book, *The Inequality of Wealth*, I was stunned to discover that someone like former prime minister Rishi Sunak had filed a tax return declaring £2 million a year – but paid just 23 per cent in tax.

Our polling with Best for Britain found that for all Reform's anti-tax rhetoric, majorities of those considering Reform back targeted levies on the wealthy and powerful to fund help with living costs. Support is strongest for windfall taxes on energy companies (64 per cent) and banks (58 per cent) that made excessive profits, alongside crackdowns on offshore tax havens (59% per cent). This anger is not ideological hostility to taxation, but a belief that the wrong people are paying – while corporations and elites escape contribution. Around 70 per cent believed income from wealth should be taxed at the same rate as income from work. Nearly half (48 per cent) support a one-off 1 per cent wealth tax on the richest 22,000 families – an extraordinary signal from a supposedly anti-tax movement.

This reminds us that to dramatise the struggle for fairness is a drama that requires antagonists. Progressives often struggle to define their enemies. Yet there is a lesson to learn from Franklin Roosevelt. Roosevelt was brilliant at not merely surviving the attacks of his opponents but thriving on them. In his famous 1936 Madison Square Garden speech he drew a clear line between the people and the powerful, attacked the 'the old enemies of peace – business and financial monopoly, speculation, reckless banking, class antagonism, sectionalism, war profiteering' and declared that 'Government by organised money is just as dangerous as Government by organised mob'.

How would we reinvent this for new times? By taking aim at 'the selfish minority'. Our polling with Best for Britain and YouGov shows us where to start; with those who don't 'play by the rules' or rip off others. At work. In the shops. In communities. Some break the law. Others break the common norms of decency. We found, for example, a deep antipathy amongst Reform voters for big business, especially energy companies and banks, whose behaviour was felt to foster a corporate greed that drove up prices and executive bonuses, and gained political influence – while families struggle. This is not a counsel for wholesale economic populism, not least because the more persuadable Reform voters are pragmatic about the virtues of big business. But by redirecting anger at profiteering, political negligence and the real cost-of-living culprits, we can undercut the populist narrative of betrayal and dump the xenophobia.

5. *A new civic gospel*

The wound which voters salve with populism is not merely an economic injury. The polling that most surprised me researching this book was the discovery that 80 per cent of hardcore Reform voters believe their area has declined – and over half say their area has declined 'a lot'; that's more than double the national average. That teaches us that populism spreads when the social foundations of belonging are destroyed and those precious ties that bind us – what sociologists call 'social capital' – are broken.

Claire Ainsley put it to me like this; the crisis for mainstream politics runs deeper than wages or living standards: 'It's partly wealth, living standards, earning power, but it's as much dignity as anything else. And status.' Claire points to a collapse of both economic and social belonging – a world where those who once 'felt they mattered, that they had status, now feel under pressure'. Community life, she notes, once offered people 'a sense of worth and visibility', but globalisation and austerity have shattered the connections that once bound neighbour to neighbour. Overwhelmingly, the most hardcore Reform voters say there isn't a good sense of community spirit in their area – a sharp contrast to other voters.

Ben Byrne's ethnographic research brings this collapse of belonging vividly to life. It describes the impotent despair at 'high streets in decline, community spaces and public spaces that were once a hubbub of community life now boarded up ... a real sense of decay and decline'. His interviewees are full of lament and anger at their communities 'shat on from a great height' and feel the loss of pride in their towns as 'soul-destroying'.

When public trust falters, family becomes the last dependable unit of belonging – the 'solace in family and neighbours' becomes 'the last safe place' in a world where community centres, shops and youth clubs have vanished. David Goodhart agreed. He described populism as a revolt of the 'Somewheres': people whose sense of worth is tied to family, local identity and place. He warns that the liberal elite has forgotten 'the moral pull of belonging', leaving many feeling that politics and culture no longer speak their language.

Successful politics, argues Goodhart, must once again 'reward loyalty to place and people'. For millions of disillusioned citizens, populism's appeal lies in its promise to restore pride in the local and the familiar – to make people feel at home again in their own country and communities. I now suspect the resonance of the populist's nostalgia is with the sense of something local that has gone.

To defeat populism, we must rebuild the home we share together with a project to restore pride in place, rebuild the spaces where people meet, and renew the ties of community life that make cooperation possible.

Once upon a time, mainstream politicians were masters of this art. On the conservative right, the idealisation of societies' 'little platoons' goes back to Edmund Burke. On the left, the labour movement was born from the idea that the individual has a better chance of realising their full potential living in a strong community. From the Rochdale pioneers of the cooperative movement to modern democratic socialism, communitarian instincts have a powerful lineage. Neil Kinnock once put it like this: 'we want a state where the collective contribution of the community is used to advance individual freedom'. Or, as Tony Blair put it later: 'The founding principle, the guiding principle of the Labour Party is the belief in community and society. It's the notion that for individuals to advance you require a strong and fair community behind you.'

Modern life snaps old bonds with new pressures. But that was true of nineteenth-century Britain when we left the farms for the factories. In his evocative memoir, the

HOW TO BEAT THEM

English playwright Laurie Lee once described the end of his village in the 1930s and with it the end of a thousand years of English history. But the response, as sociologist Robert Putnam explains, was not a horrified return to the manor but an explosion in civic energy. What became known as the civic gospel built Britain's great town halls, churches and faith movements, municipal companies, sports clubs, youth movements and trade unions.

That is exactly the spirit we need today. A refreshed fraternity. A renewed civic gospel. And that must start by creating the safety to come together, without which community life is impossible – a lack of safety encourages us to retreat to our homes and proverbially raise the drawbridge.

Our polling found that more than half of those considering voting Reform said boosting the local police was their top priority for improving their community. A further 45 per cent called for harsher rules on theft. Safety and order are the cornerstones of renewing local civic life and when we examine what unites persuadable Reform voters and 'left-bloc' voters, there's one clear priority: the fight to bring our high streets back to life.

The high street has become a symbol, a cipher for the state of local society. When people talk about boarded-up shops, they're talking about safety, about pride, about whether anyone still cares about the place they call home. Revive the high street and we have our symbols of a moral restoration of order and dignity, a visible statement that we still believe in community.

Rebuilding pride of place is every bit as central to defeating populism as raising pay or reforming the state. Knit that together with a stronger family policy and we have the makings of a renewed belonging. When people are not ashamed of the state of the street on which they live, when they have a neighbourhood where they're proud to bring their family and friends, we have a new defence against extremists. And if we can't give people back a sense of home, the populists will. Rebuilding communities is a test case of whether we have a state that can deliver or – as we might put it better – a state that can perform.

6. Performance

Populism is nourished by a hardening sense that politics no longer works for ordinary people. A healthy scepticism has curdled into angry contempt. In the UK, those considering Reform feel not apathy about politicians but disgust. They see Westminster as a closed club run by people who 'have never done a proper job'. An extraordinary 86 per cent of the most hardcore Reform voters say tax money is wasted and spent on the wrong things. As one local resident put it to me, 'They all talk about change, but nothing changes – not for us.'

It is understandable. The litany of state failures in Britain – from major scandals like the post-office scandal to huge cost overruns on any major project like HS2, to small boats endlessly crossing the channel – fills books. Productivity in our National Health Service is so bad, it actually drags the nation's overall productivity growth into negative numbers. Amongst the best surveys is *Failed State*, written by policy specialist Sam Freedman. He argues that the problem is not merely who is in charge but how the system is designed. In Britain we have a highly centralised power-structure that actually lacks any levers to deliver. In

Sam's words: 'You've got this unbelievably powerful presidential figure who has very few resources ... this mismatch means ... very bad policy development from the centre of government.'

Many now trust populists to name the disease and so trust them to prescribe the cure. The hunger for honesty is so intense that bluntness is taken for truth. Populists' plain talk cuts through because, in a culture of evasion, clarity feels radical. Populism presents itself as truth-telling – risky, raw and real. So it is not enough for mainstream politics simply to 'win the argument'. We have to prove that the state can actually get things done.

That means more than simply delivery; it means performance.[13] American political theorist William Galston explains this well. In his book *Anger, Fear, Domination*,[14] he explains that today's erosion of trust stems from three failures of performance: lack of delivery, broken promises and unnecessary wars. Populists, by contrast, are perceived to 'do what they said they'd do'. Citizens lose faith not because they reject democracy's ideals, but because they no longer believe its institutions can act. Credibility shifts to those who seem to perform – even if the performance is reckless – because in an age of paralysis, action – any action – becomes proof that some sort of agency is still possible. President Trump's promise – and action – to 'stop the border' and 'put tariffs on' can all be debated but arguably, the act of keeping his promises built Trump's credibility.

I have seen first-hand how centralised control and bureaucratic inertia destroy performance. Transforming performance will prove impossible without a bold programme to devolve power and resources out of Whitehall and reinvent what's left. But that is not quite enough.

Ben Page put it to me bluntly: if 'everybody thinks the state is broken', then 'tangible delivery moments are absolutely what you need'. People do not feel GDP. They do not feel structural reforms or five-year plans. They feel whether the bus turns up, whether the A&E queue is shorter, whether the high street is thriving, whether we've stopped the parking on verges, chaos outside schools at pick-up time and street-racers tearing through the quiet of the night.

The lesson is clear. Politicians should focus on 'signal' policies that are impossible to miss – the things you can point at in a street and say, 'That changed.' Dramatic interventions – saving a steel plant, reopening a walk-in centre, restoring a local police station – resonate more deeply than a dozen incremental tweaks, because they create memorable images that challenge the narrative of decline.

Yet even that is not quite enough. As Alison Phillips reminded me, politics is not a performance review. It is an emotional relationship. Too often, she argues, politicians might deliver real change but then fail to claim it. They risk endlessly talking about problems while whispering about progress.

Her prescription is simple: 'Celebrate it, celebrate your achievements, make sure people know about it.' Joy, she says, is a political weapon. Victories, no matter how modest, should be celebrated in a way that reassures people that progress is happening and that they have a stake in it. Tangible delivery is necessary but insufficient. It must be visible, relatable and celebrated – transformed from policy wins into emotional wins, moments that resonate in the gut as well as the head.

If mainstream leaders tell the story of Britain in the minor key of austerity, warnings and hardship, they will leave populists to offer the only emotional release on offer: anger, blame and grievance.

The task, then, is to turn the state from a symbol of failure into a visible instrument of success: a government that fixes the basics and is proud of it. Leaders who don't just apologise for what is broken but stand in front of what has been repaired and say: this works again – and we did it together.

Without progress, pride, optimism, order and effectiveness, it will be very hard to win. With them, we can begin to break the spell of state failure on which populism feeds – and prove that democracy can still deliver for those who have every reason to doubt it.

7. Fight kleptocracy not just populism

It will prove hard to defeat populism unless we disrupt the spigots of cash that flow to populist politicians, parties and their allies in the kleptosphere.

Among the many ironies of modern politics is the truth that populist voters, convinced the market is rigged against them, vote for populist politicians who make more money out of politics that almost anyone else.

In my research decoding populism, I heard voters tell me time and time again that 'people like me don't get our fair share', 'the rich and powerful always win', 'the system's fixed'. And they have a point. The lesson that populist voters draw is that we need a strong leader to clean the proverbial stables. Over 60 per cent of hardcore Reform voters strongly agree with the idea that 'we need a strong leader to take the country back from the rich and powerful'. This is not a revolt against democracy. It is a cry to clean up democracy.

Yet those who promise loudest to 'drain the swamp' are all too often those who dig it deeper – and drown the evidence. The historian Christian Goeschel warned me that this is how corruption always starts: 'Whenever populists take power at the local level ... you immediately begin to find corruption.' From Hungary to Poland to Austria, he said, the pattern is identical: 'They siphon state money into private projects ... create oligarchs who control the media ... and divert public funds to friends and family.' Populism, in other words, is not just ideology; it is a business model built on patronage.

Around the world, today's authoritarian populists are now perfecting what Anne Applebaum calls 'a new business model for kleptocracy'. The tragedy of this perverted innovation is that some of the smartest Western financiers helped write the kleptocrats' playbook. As Applebaum put it to me, this is 'a world of kleptocracy co-created by the West and the East ... half us and half them'. The risk, Applebaum warns, is that 'the differences between the so-called Western democracies and the autocratic world are shrinking [because] ... they're interactive'. Western banks and law firms built the machinery – the offshore havens, anonymous shell companies, and dark-money networks – and autocrats simply learned how to weaponise it.

Britain is deeply implicated in this world. Our financial system has become one of the world's great laundromats; ministers admit there is a realistic possibility that the scale of money-laundering through the UK is hundreds of billions of pounds every year: a proverbial haystack in which to hide some dirty needles.

That leaves our political system vulnerable to old techniques that shift dark money onshore into the bank accounts of British citizens from which it can be safely donated and swapped for influence with political parties or politicians. Dark donors can all too easily create 'Alka-Seltzer companies' that can be set up, can donate money and then disappear or dissolve. These are easily connected to a global ecosystem of unregulated influence: replicas of foreign think tanks bankrolled by foreign companies with super-sized influence and no scrutiny to go with it.

But the kleptosphere never sleeps. And now it has new tools to play with: digital media and cryptocurrency.

Digital media systems can channel cash to politicians without really disclosing its original source. And this can be a lot of money. As we saw in Chapter 7, we were able to trace some £153 million across just four years pouring into Britain's populist media-political complex, funded, by and large, by just four people. Yet much of this money flowed through opaque corporate webs: like Legatum's Dubai HQ with accounts that are filed in the British Virgin Islands. The effect is corrosive. Outlets like GB News don't just platform populism; they pay for it. Reform's MPs bank the fees. And the line between public duty and private gain blurs ever further.

Cryptocurrency is an even bigger risk. Many American voters believe that President Trump's innovative use of cryptocurrency to sell meme coins with no intrinsic value is super-smart. But I fear it will soon inspire other leaders to create pseudo-firms that enable the powerful to pay tributes to politicians not in gold but in untraceable crypto-tokens. 'I'd be amazed,' Anne added, 'if [this model is] not copied by other people ... Erdoğan, or President Le Pen – why wouldn't you do that too?'

We should be worried by what we can see already. Crypto firms – with owners in places like the BVI and Guernsey – are already sponsoring political-party conferences. A march led by Tommy Robinson was backed by a crypto company under investigation in America.[15]

Worse, corruption may be about to go algorithmic. Artificial intelligence could soon be used to make thousands of cryptocurrency payments below the thresholds for public declarations. In a matter of seconds, code could move hundreds of thousands of dark pounds into the digital wallets of politicians or their proxies. Algorithmic corruption could hijack politics faster than we can modernise the law.

Surely we should not allow innovations in political finance that we cannot police? Until enforcement catches up, cryptocurrency donations to political parties should be banned. We should outlaw paid media roles for sitting MPs and require full disclosure of offshore and foreign funding. We should arm election watchdogs with real enforcement powers and close the loopholes that let shell companies sluice money through think tanks and conferences. Down the years, too many populist leaders have learned to speak the language of the people while looting the institutions of the state. Our task is to expose the lie – and prove that a democracy scrubbed clean of kleptocracy can once again be the people's best defence against the powerful.

8. *The patriotism of our best ideals*

Roosevelt's inauguration speech in 1933 redefined American patriotism for new times. He re-imagined patriotism as a moral covenant: courage over fear, service over selfishness, unity over division, decency over despair. He defined a patriotism of the country's best ideals. And to defeat populism today, that is exactly what we must do once more: set out the patriotism of our true ideals that define these isles of wonder.

Populists win not because their ideas are coherent, but because their stories are simple. As we have seen, they tell a three-chord tale of belonging and betrayal, of patriotism, nostalgia and urgency. But their patriotism is narrow, their nostalgia selective, and their urgency little more than anger in disguise. They wave cheap Union Jacks made in China, hymn the national anthem but forget the second verse, and promise to 'make the nation great again' with nothing more than soundbites. They'll defend your liberty for about as long as you agree with them and not a second more. They'll say that they alone defend tradition and carry the torch of national renewal. Yet the point is not who defends our history. Wisdom is discerning what is best about our history that is worth conserving.

Our patriotism must mean not just a duty but a promise – the promise of a people who, through struggle and solidarity, enlarged the meaning of freedom for all. Ours is the patriotism of Magna Carta and Mill, of Wilberforce and the suffragettes, of miners' banners and the NHS. It is not the politics of 'us and them', but of all of us together. We reject the exclusive patriotism that trades on hatred. We believe, as Charles de Gaulle put it, 'Patriotism is when love of your own people comes first; nationalism, when hate for people other than your own comes first.' We choose love.

Nor must we mistake a reverence for the past with a desire to live there. As John Stuart Mill warned, 'The despotism of custom is everywhere the standing hindrance to human advancement.' The godfather of communitarian thinking Amitai Etzioni once joked that the 1950s were safe – 'and God-awful', because life in the 1950s marginalised women, minorities and anyone who dared to be different.

One of the single best thinkers on this is Sunder Katwala, founder and chief executive of British Future, whose superb book *How to Be a Patriot* is a must read.[16] Sunder argues that the antidote to the populist hijacking of patriotism lies not in abandoning patriotism but in reclaiming it. As he put it, populists succeed because 'the vocal populist minority has got a confidence about how to speak in a very resonant way to a third of our society' while the 'pluralist, nuanced, anti-populist majority' lacks 'a clarity or confidence about its voice and its agenda other than "we don't like populism"'.

That, he suggests, leaves mainstream politics afraid to talk about belonging, nationhood and fairness – terrain populists then seize. So what is needed is an inclusive story of nationhood – a generous patriotism – that joins pride with fairness; a patriotism of civic decency rather than cultural exclusion. It rests on a belief that Britain works best when contribution and compassion walk hand in hand. If populists weaponise patriotism to divide, the cure is not to retreat but to speak of belonging with courage and love.

In this, tradition is our friend. Traditions are not in fact static; they evolve generation after generation. Our challenge is not to walk away from tradition, but 'to update the story so everyone can see themselves inside it'. The rituals that once bound us – from Remembrance to royal jubilees, from the NHS to the village fête – should and could become open acts of belonging in which new Britons are not spectators but participants. Tradition, in this sense, is not a cold inheritance but a living invitation: a way of saying that the nation's story is still being written, and everyone has a line to add. When patriotism becomes a shared stage instead of a closed circle, the flag – or, even better, bunting – stops being a symbol of fear and starts becoming a banner of fellowship.

Over 20 years of public life, I've spent countless hours talking to people about what they love about our country. You often hear a brilliant list of old favourites. Beer in a decent pub. Fashion and fish and chips. Our stunning countryside, chocolate, cider, our seasons and our sense of humour. The great English language. Family, friends, friendliness and football. Law and order, common sense, community spirit. The Royals and rugby. Good manners, queueing and a nice cup of tea. All the things you'd miss if you were scooped up and plonked on a desert island.

But what has struck me down the years is how ten ideals form a kind of British Decalogue – the commandments of a civic faith that made liberty our birthright: the foundations of freedom, the bonds of belonging.

The foundations of freedom are the civic bedrock that secures liberty, starting with the rule of law. From Magna Carta to habeas corpus, from the Bill of Rights to the Human Rights Act, our freedom has always been secured by law not whim. We are a people who believe in rules because rules protect the weak from the strong.

Second is our scientific, rational empirical spirit. We are the home of the Scientific Revolution, a nation that has buried its scientists with our sovereigns since the death of

Isaac Newton. We are children of Newton and Darwin, of Ada Lovelace, Alan Turing and Tim Berners-Lee. The curiosity that has driven this exploration of ideas has animated our exploration of the world. We have always been outward-looking islands. Little England has never been our tradition. Ours is the country that sailed, traded, explored and built bonds across the world. Our story is one of bridges – a global outlook grounded in curiosity not fear.

Perhaps it's our reason and love of law that fosters our radicalism about power: the idea that no one can tell us what to do. We are an ancient radical nation. From the barons who tamed the king to the Levellers, the Chartists and the suffragettes, we have always demanded that power serve the people. Ours is the country that invented the social contract, not the divine right of kings. These three ideals – liberty safeguarded by law, reason over dogma, power that is checked – define the British constitutional temperament.

The bonds of belonging are the social virtues that knit us together. First among them is tolerance. We are, at heart, a live-and-let-live people. Our tolerance is why we love eccentrics and why John Stuart Mill could build a whole philosophy around 'experiments in living'. As a multi-faith, multi-nation, multi-colour country born from the Reformation, the Act of Union and the British Empire, we have long learned that tolerance is what turns difference into strength. It is what allows us to laugh at ourselves and still live together.

Next is compassion. Our hearts are softer than the old stiff upper lip suggests. The 'Blitz spirit' and the NHS sprang from the same instincts – the instinct of fellowship, that we are 'our brother's keeper'. Compassion is not weakness. It is courage in action. It is why the NHS and the welfare state remain amongst the institutions people are proudest of – because they express our moral imagination in the real world.

Perhaps that compassion is why we love an underdog – and hate bullies. From Wilberforce to Churchill, from the suffragettes to the anti-apartheid marches, we have stood with the weak against the strong. We take pride in backing the little guy – at home or abroad. We are not perfect but, when bullies rise, our instinct is to resist. These virtues express the emotional core of British life: decency, duty and everyday solidarity.

A love and flair for the creative hearth is also part of the national character. So often our patriotism is expressed through local tradition, from the National Eisteddfod to Burns Night, to the Durham Miners' Gala, to Lewes Bonfire Night, our local loyalties are the heart of our national life. Patriotism does not smother local identity; it celebrates it. When people speak of what they love about our country, they talk about their town, their team, their traditions. National renewal begins on the village green and civic square.

We are also a nation which tolerates mediocrity – but loves beauty. Despite the ugliness of too many towns, we believe that beauty belongs to everyone. From Bournville to Bath, from William Morris to Port Sunlight, we built beauty for all, not just for the rich. The belief that decency demands dignity in our surroundings is a quiet, radical creed.

Finally, we are a nation shaped by nature – the green and pleasant land of Blake's anthem. The love of gardens, the care for the countryside, the fight for clean air and green space are all acts of patriotism. They are expressions of gratitude to the land that shaped us and a duty to those who will inherit it.

These are not relics; they make up the patriotism of our best ideals. True patriotism is not about waving the flag but about honouring what it stands for – fairness, decency, duty, freedom and courage. Yet patriotism of our true beliefs is not nostalgia; it is a compass. It is the promise of our country – and the promise we must renew.

9. *The permanent dialogue*

It was President Lyndon Johnson who said, 'what convinces is conviction'. Populists are conviction politicians. They cut through the digital fog that smothers modern life. They are masters of the medium because they are masters of its logic – simplicity, repetition, rage. Their slogans are short, vivid, moral, human. They tell serial stories that unfold week by week like soap operas. They understand that, in the digital arena, emotion outruns reason. Yet the online battle to defeat populism can be waged in three ways.

First, as Alison Phillips argues, mainstream politics must rediscover the language of feeling as well as fact. Populists win, she says, because they 'communicate on an emotional, moral level' – they make people laugh, cry or rage, while mainstream leaders sound managerial and joyless. When leaders give people reasons to feel proud again – when they tell moral stories of decency, effort and renewal – they re-energise hope. The antidote to grievance politics, she concludes, is celebration politics: delivery you can feel.

But digital politics must be more than new craft – it must be a new conversation. In the late 1990s the last great progressive campaign innovator was Bill Clinton. He mastered what became known as the 'permanent campaign',[17] a campaign mindset that became a style of governing. 'Governing', said experts at the time, became 'indistinguishable from running for office'. Voter surveys were used 'in perpetual fashion'. Speeches were polled 'word by word, line by line, phrase by phrase, paragraph by paragraph'. Political consultants were put in high office. Fundraising was pervasive.

Today, populists have re-invented the game once more. They are not merely in a permanent campaign. They are in a permanent dialogue. Mornings are spent immersed in the nation's digital souks so that, by the time they roll into the office, they know what the nation thinks. To beat populists, mainstream leaders must reclaim this lost art of conversation. Politics cannot be an occasional broadcast; the permanent campaign must become the permanent dialogue. Leaders must be seen taking criticism, arguing their case, shaping a continuous story of progress: fairness, pride, opportunity – illustrated by tangible change.

It is not as novel as it sounds. Early in his New Deal years Franklin Roosevelt began receiving hundreds of thousands of letters a week. He did not ignore them. He turned them into a political resource. His staff would summarise, parse and pass on verbatim passages. Roosevelt then used these voices – 'letters from the people' – as proof that his policies were grounded in the struggles of ordinary Americans. He lived in dialogue with the nation. Phrases like 'Many of you have written to me …' or 'I have had thousands of letters from farmers and workers who tell me …' transformed a one-way radio broadcast into the sense of a two-way conversation. Just as Roosevelt mastered the radio, so today's leaders must master the algorithm. But they must use the technology of our age not to monetise rage but to mobilise reason.

These efforts are more likely to succeed if we get serious about tackling the platforms that supercharge division. In today's digital archipelago, outrage is rewarded because outrage pays. We have watched some of the richest men on the planet build a distortion field that corrodes democratic debate. Bad actors exploit it, coordinating mass shares of hashtagged content, re-shared at scale to trigger algorithmic amplification. It is not a marketplace of ideas. It is a casino of emotion, rigged by design.

We must defend the right to free speech. But there is no human right to amplification. A Rooseveltian plan for the digital age would both democratise communication and discipline the platforms that corrode democracy. It would pair a renaissance of civic storytelling with the regulation of a toxic business model. That means algorithmic transparency, duty-of-care obligations and independent auditing. Platforms that magnify lies and hate should not be rewarded for it.

This is not censorship – it is common sense. When, as the House of Commons warns, 'foreign powers … coordinate disinformation' or domestic extremists weaponise social media to intimidate minorities and elected representatives alike, we must act. We would not let foreign agents buy television networks to broadcast propaganda unchallenged. Neither should we let digital networks profiteer from unregulated division.

10. Lead with courage, not caution

The future is still unwritten. But the parallels with the late 1920s should alarm us. After the 1929 Wall Street crash, democracies teetered as the Great Depression bit. Hard times bred anger, anger fuelled extremism and, confronted with extremists, the defenders of democracy all too often faltered.

In Weimar Germany, exhausted by inflation, humiliation and political paralysis, moderation became meekness. As historian Christian Goeschel reminds us, the tragedy of Weimar was not only the audacity of its enemies, but the timidity of its defenders. The Social Democrats 'should have been so much more courageous in promoting the Weimar Republic ... in fighting against the Nazis'. Instead, they trusted that legal norms would protect liberty, and bureaucracy would save democracy.

That is the lesson history offers with pitiless clarity: robust defence of liberalism cannot be left to legal process or half-measures. It must be fought for boldly or it will be lost. Caution is no protection against those who thrive on chaos. It was boldness that saved democracy in the 1930s, not bureaucracy – and it was Franklin Roosevelt who showed how.

When Roosevelt took office in 1933, extremists were marching across Europe, the banks were collapsing and a quarter of Americans were unemployed. But he refused to kowtow to the politics of fear. His words still light the path: 'The only thing we have to fear is fear itself.'

Roosevelt did more than offer honeyed words to comfort a wounded people. He understood that the battle against despair could not be won with speeches alone. It had to be fought with pay packets, on farms and high streets, in homes. He launched the New Deal not as a soundbite but as a covenant between government and the governed – a promise that that democracy would deliver dignity, work and security for all.

In that covenant lay his genius. Roosevelt did not out-shout extremists, he out-performed them. He made government work again so people could believe again. He transformed anger into agency and despair into determination. In Roosevelt's hands, delivery became the national story of democracy – a fireside tale told from one man to millions. In doing so, he re-armed democracy with justice – proving that progress need not mean disorder, and that freedom without fairness means little.

That is the challenge before us now. We live once more in an age of economic disillusionment, technological upheaval and political fatigue. Populists thrive on this exhaustion. They promise clarity amid chaos, and strength amid stagnation. They weaponise fear – of decline, of outsiders, of loss. But as Roosevelt showed, the antidote to fear is courage, and courage can be contagious. What people need is not anger but agency – the sense that the system works, that change is possible, and that progress is still possible for them.

Roosevelt reborn today would offer more than nostalgia for the New Deal of the past. He would offer a new deal for the age of AI: rebuilding trust through visible fairness, good work, and institutions that serve the many, not the few. Just as Roosevelt re-forged America's faith in democracy through public works and social reform, we need a new security on which to build opportunity: secure jobs, green energy, fair taxes, universal digital access, and education systems that equip everyone to thrive in the age of AI.

Courage, not caution, must guide this effort. The centre cannot win by trimming its sails to the winds of fear. It must once again tell an audacious, patriotic story that joins freedom to fairness – a story that reaches the heart as well as the head. That means talking about values as well as numbers, celebrating delivery as well as diagnosing decline. Roosevelt was a master storyteller because he understood that emotion and evidence must work together. He spoke to the heart but acted with the head. He built faith through results – jobs, homes, pensions, roads – each a symbol that democracy worked.

If today's progressives are to prevail, we must do the same. We must out-perform, out-communicate and out-moralise the populists. We must turn politics back into a promise kept – a promise that fairness will be visible and that government will work for those who play by the rules.

The message of Weimar is that democracy dies when its defenders lose their nerve. The message of Roosevelt is that it lives when they find their courage. That is where a new story must start, with courage over caution, justice over fear, and the radical centre proving, once again, that democracy can deliver.

Roosevelt showed that hope, when coupled with action, can transform a nation. Today, mainstream politics must connect with the surge tide of anger that powers the populist rise, and rebuild a radical centre of Western liberalism. We cannot simply take shelter from the storm. We must sail the tempest.

Acknowledgements

This book brings together an extraordinary range of research, reflection and conversations that have unfolded in the years since I published *The Inequality of Wealth*. This is, essentially, the politics of the economics I set out in that book. But to write *Why Populists Are Winning*, I incurred immense debts to an exceptional group of people across the UK, Europe and the United States who helped shape my thinking, challenge my assumptions, or simply gave generously of their time and thoughts.

A great deal of this thinking was developed at St Antony's College, Oxford, where, as a Visiting Parliamentary Fellow, I was lucky enough to co-host with Rt Hon John Glen MP a series of seminars on 'Good Policy in the Age of Populism'. I am immensely grateful to Professor Roger Goodman, Warden of the College, for his encouragement, and to the remarkable thinkers who came to speak including Professor Ngaire Woods, Lord Mark Malloch Brown, Sir John Sawers, Air Marshal (Ret'd) Edward Stringer, Jon Sopel, Kelly Beaver, Alison Phillips, Tim Montgomerie, Desmond King, Roy Allison, Helen Margetts, Matthew Taylor, Nick Markham, Malcolm Gooderham and Lazlo Varro, who offered clear-eyed wisdom at a moment when clarity is in short supply.

As you would expect for a book with deep roots in political science research, I have been blessed to be able

ACKNOWLEDGEMENTS

to draw on the advice and research of some of the best thinkers in the field. In particular, I had the privilege of working with Best for Britain, and its brilliant Chief Executive Naomi Smith; Professor Bobby Duffy and the team at the Policy Institute, King's College London along with Patrick English and his team at YouGov and research agency Faster Horses, led by Ben Byrne, whose insights into the lives and frustrations of Britain's populist tribes proved indispensable.

Analysing the data we gathered would have been impossible without the help of Rick Foster, Mansfield College, Oxford, who also made a huge contribution to the original work on semantic analysis, along with invaluable background research by Hannah Bulmer.

Much of the framework for my thinking I owe to Professor Jane Green, Nuffield College, who guided me during my time with the college, enriched by lots of time spent with some of the country's leading political scientists and polling specialists, in particular Peter Kellner, Ben Page, Kelly Beaver, Professor Ben Ansell (Nuffield), Professor Anthony King, and Professor Pepper Culpepper (Blavatnik).

Across Europe and beyond, I benefited enormously from discussions with leaders, thinkers and writers who have witnessed the populist wave close up, including Claire Ainsley, Dame Deborah Mattinson, Will Marshall and Lindsay Lewis at PPI, and Josh Freed and the team at Third Way. Peter Hyman has been a huge influence on the conclusions at which I arrived and a forceful debate partner throughout the project, along with Sunder Katwala at British Future, Dan Turner, David Goodhart, Alastair Campbell and Dr Christian Goeschel to whom

ACKNOWLEDGEMENTS

I'm especially grateful for insights into 1920s Germany. Both Chris Mason and Jon Sopel were generous in sharing scrupulously independent insights and stories from their ring-side seats reporting on American politics.

This book also draws on many conversations and research from my work on the House of Commons Joint Committee on the National Security Strategy, and its work on defending democracy. Over years I've drawn heavily on my work together with Dame Margaret Hodge, Oliver Bullough, Duncan Hames and Peter Geoghegan, who each helped illuminate different corners of the global 'impunity industry' and crucially, to Anne Applebaum, whose work on autocracy and corruption has shaped my understanding more than she knows. Adam Bychawski was instrumental in helping assemble my research work to support my role on the Committee and prepare for the UK's Elections Bill. Alan Jagolinzer was generous enough to share insights from his work around the Cambridge Disinformation Summit. James Bloodworth helped me understand the manosphere, while the ethical data science company Signify were generous in sharing their analysis on today's online populist echo-chambers.

Finally, profound thanks go to my agent Georgina Capel, who first suggested the idea of this book and the brilliant team at Head of Zeus led by Holly Harley, along with my London office expertly helmed by the indefatigable Olivia Coyle. None of this work or these words could have been produced without the infinite patience and wisdom and nudge in the right direction of my wife, Sarah.

This book is, in its heart, an attempt to draw coherence from the hundreds of conversations I have had in recent

ACKNOWLEDGEMENTS

years – on doorsteps, in community centres, in union halls, in universities, in parliaments and in private rooms where people wrestle with a simple question: 'how does mainstream politics renew?' Those conversations – often raw, sometimes angry, always honest – have shaped this book more than any seminar or study. To everyone who shared their experiences, their doubts and their hopes: thank you. The errors, misjudgments and omissions are, of course, entirely my own.

Notes

1 The Age of Rage

1. Manuel Funke, Moritz Schularick and Christoph Trebesch, 'Populist Leaders and the Economy', *American Economic Review* 113, no. 12 (Dec. 2023), pp. 3249–88, https://doi.org/10.1257/aer.20202045
2. See J. Cliffe, T. Coratella, C. Lons and A. Varvelli, 'Rise to the challengers: Europe's populist parties and its foreign policy future' (policy brief) (12 Jun. 2025).
3. The hard-right Patriots for Europe and the European Conservatives and Reformists.
4. In 2024, Reform polled 4.1 million votes (14.3 per cent), five MPs, and second place in 98 constituencies.
5. Cas Mudde and Cristobal Rovira Kaltwasser, *Populism: A Very Short Introduction* (Very Short Introductions), (Oxford University Press, 2017) Kindle edn.
6. Personally I think the definition of 'authoritarian populism' is well defined in Míriam Juan-Torres González, 'Fear, Grievance, and the Other: How Authoritarian Populist Politics Thrive in Contemporary Democracies – Key Concepts to Understand Politics Beyond the Left-Right Paradigm', Primer: Othering & Belonging Institute, University of California, Berkeley, 2024. The application of the concept was originated by Stuart Hall. See Stuart Hall, 'The Great Moving Right Show', *Marxism Today*, 14–20 Jan. 1979.
7. E. J. Hobsbawm, 'The Machine Breakers', *Past & Present* (1952) 1 (1), pp. 57–70.
8. International Monetary Fund, 'World Must Prioritize Productivity Reforms to Revive Medium-Term Growth', *IMF Blog*, 10 Apr. 2024, https://www.imf.org/en/Blogs/Articles/2024/04/10/world-must-prioritize-productivity-reforms-to-revive-medium-term-growth (accessed 2 Feb. 2026).

NOTES

9 Author calculations based on House of Commons library data assembling IMF growth rates and Freedom House data, https://freedomhouse.org/explore-the-map?type=fiw&year=2025. Between 2010 and 2025, annual GDP growth rates in countries classed as 'free' in 2025 grew on average 2.5 per cent/year between 2010 and 2025, compared to 3.1 per cent in countries classed as 'not free'.

10 Pew Research Center, 'False Information Seen as a Major Threat Worldwide, as Are Terrorism, Disease and the Global Economy; Climate Change Is Now Mostly a Secondary Concern', Washington, DC, 18 Aug. 2025, https://www.pewresearch.org/global/2025/08/19/international-opinion-on-global-threats/pg_2025-08-19_global-threats_0_03/ (accessed 2 Feb. 2026).

11 Policy Institute, King's College London, and Ipsos UK, 'The UK's Changing "Culture Wars": Division, Tension and Common Ground', Nov. 2025.

12 World Bank, World Development Report 2023: 'Migrants, Refugees, and Societies', pp. 46–50, 121, 161, 272.

13 Kristalina Georgieva, 'AI Will Transform the Global Economy. Let's Make Sure It Benefits Humanity', *IMF Blog*, 14 Jan. 2024, https://www.imf.org/en/Blogs/Articles/2024/01/14/ai-will-transform-the-global-economy-lets-make-sure-it-benefits-humanity (accessed 2 Feb. 2026).

14 Daron Acemoglu and James A. Robinson, *The Narrow Corridor: States, Societies, and the Fate of Liberty* (New York: Penguin Press, 2019).

15 In this delicate space, the Leviathan of the state was created but 'shackled' so it remains strong enough to govern and keep peace, but is, Acemoglu and Robinson argue, 'shackled by common people, by norms, and by institutions – in short by society'. As Acemoglu and Robinson conclude: 'If they [state and society] work within the corridor, they can increase the capacities of both state and society. But … they can become polarized and zero-sum', ibid. p. 420.

16 Funke, Schularick and Trebesch, ibid.

17 Richard Overy, *The Morbid Age: Britain and the Crisis of Civilisation, 1919–1939* (London: Penguin Books, 2010).

18 Evans, *The Coming of the Third Reich*, p. 324.

19 Ibid. p. 594.

2 Meet the Populists

1. A phrase introduced by the late great Peter Mair in his book *Ruling the Void: The Hollowing of Western Democracy* (London & New York: Verso, 2013).
2. President Donald Trump won just 31.43 per cent of *registered voters* in the 2024 US presidential election.
3. An insight I owe to Professor Vincent Pons at the Harvard Business School.
4. T. Piketty, A. Gethin and C. Martínez-Toledano, 'Brahmin Left versus Merchant Right: Changing Political Cleavages in 21 Western Democracies, 1948–2020', *Quarterly Journal of Economics*, 137(1) (2022).
5. Piketty, ibid. p. 30.
6. Ezra Klein, *Why We're Polarized* (Profile, 2020), Kindle edn.
7. Carnegie Endowment for International Peace, 'Polarization, Democracy, and Political Violence in the United States: What the Research Says' (Sep. 2023), available at https://carnegieendowment.org/research/2023/09/polarization-democracy-and-political-violence-in-the-united-states-what-the-research-says (accessed 2 Feb. 2026).
8. Pew Research Center, 'Most across 19 countries see strong partisan conflicts in their society, especially in South Korea and the U.S.' (Nov. 2022), available at www.pewresearch.org/short-reads/2022/11/16/most-across-19-countries-see-strong-partisan-conflicts-in-their-society-especially-in-south-korea-and-the-u-s (accessed 2 Feb. 2025).
9. Tony Blair Institute for Global Change, 'Disruptive Delivery: Meeting the Unmet Demand in Politics' (January 2025), available at https://institute.global/insights/politics-and-governance/disruptive-delivery-meeting-the-unmet-demand-in-politics (accessed 2 Feb. 2026).
10. Defined as Marine Le Pen's National Rally in France, Reform UK in Britain, Alternative for Germany (AfD) and Canada's People's Party.
11. This group, which represents 14 per cent of our sample, includes better-off supporters of Donald Trump in the United States, voters for the Conservative Party in Canada, and backers of the Christian Social Union in Germany.
12. George Dangerfield, *The Strange Death of Liberal England* (1935), p. 70.
13. As indeed, some have tried. See for instance Geoffrey Wheatcroft, *The Strange Death of Tory England* (2005).
14. Pew Research Center, 'Behind Trump's 2024 Victory, a More Racially and Ethnically Diverse Voter Coalition' (June 2025), available at https://www.pewresearch.org/politics/2025/06/26/behind-trumps-

2024-victory-a-more-racially-and-ethnically-diverse-voter-coalition/ (accessed 2 Feb. 2026).

15 See Jane Green and Marta Miori, 'The Reform Revolution: An End to Two-party Politics or Its Reinvention?' (2025), available at https://politicscentre.nuffield.ox.ac.uk/opinion/the-reform-revolution/ (accessed 2 Feb. 2026). Only 5 per cent of 2024 Labour voters saw Reform as their preferred (more 'liked') party among those they didn't vote for. Even as 2025 wore on and the Labour government began to struggle, only 10 per cent of Labour voters were defecting to Reform.

16 Cited in Persuasion UK, 'Getting to Know "Reform curious Labour Voters"' (Apr. 2025).

17 38 Degrees; private briefing (2025).

18 Persuasion UK, 'Getting to Know "Reform curious Labour Voters"' (Apr. 2025). While some 11 per cent of 2024 Labour voters are currently 'open' to voting Reform (rising to 18 per cent in Scotland), these numbers are dwarfed by Labour voters considering defections to the Greens (29 per cent) or Lib Dems (41 per cent).

19 As Norris and Inglehart put it, Trump's supporters were socially conservative. They reported: 'The evidence confirms ... that Trump's support was concentrated among socially conservative, older white men, non-college graduates, and residents in small-town America, especially Republicans endorsing authoritarian values.' These trends are long-standing. 'Indeed,' the *New York Times* commentator Ezra Klein noted, 'most people who voted chose the same party in 2016 that they'd chosen in 2012', Ezra Klein, *Why We're Polarized* (Profile, 2020), Kindle edn.

20 Thomas Piketty, 'Brahmin Left vs Merchant Right: Rising Inequality & the Changing Structure of Political Conflict', PSE Working Paper, 2018, Paris: Paris School of Economics.

21 D. Rodrik, 'Why Does Globalization Fuel Populism? Economics, Culture, and the Rise of Right-Wing Populism', *Annual Review of Economics*, 13: 133–70 (Aug. 2021), available at www.annualreviews.org/content/journals/10.1146/annurev-economics-070220-032416 (accessed 2 Feb. 2026).

22 Piketty et al, 'Brahmin Left versus Merchant Right: Changing Political Cleavages in 21 Western Democracies, 1948–2020', *Quarterly Journal of Economics*, 137(1) (2022).

23 Matthijs Rooduijn, 'What unites the voter bases of populist parties? Comparing the electorates of 15 populist parties', Aug. 2018, pp. 351–68. See also M. Rooduijn, 'The rise of the populist radical right in Western

NOTES

Europe', *European View*, 14(1) (2015), pp. 3–11, https://doi.org/10.1007/s12290-015-0347-5

24 George Orwell, *The Lion and the Unicorn: Socialism and the English Genius* (Secker & Warburg, 1941) (Part I: 'England Your England').

25 The quotes in the next set of pen portraits are drawn from this work. See Faster Horses (2025), 'Decoding Populism: Uncovering Britain's Epidemic of Discontent – An Ethnographic Exploration' (Summary Report) available at https://static1.squarespace.com/static/5ecfec9a27d97a01fe2c9617/t/68888716c5daa66a7a2297e4/1753777942431/Decoding+Populism+-+Headline+Report+(Aug+2025).pdf (accessed 2 Feb. 2026).

3 The End of Hope

1 Francis Fukuyama, *The End of History and the Last Man* (New York: Free Press, 1992).
2 Bill Clinton, 'World without walls', *Guardian*, 26 Jan. 2002,
3 Evelyne Hübscher and Thomas Sattler, forthcoming, cited in 'Fear the Deficit-Populism Doom Loop', *Economist*, 24 Aug. 2025.
4 Sascha O. Becker, Thiemo Fetzer and Dennis Novy, 'Who Voted for Brexit? A Comprehensive District-Level Analysis', CEP Discussion Paper No. 1480 (2017), London: Centre for Economic Performance, London School of Economics and Political Science, https://cep.lse.ac.uk/pubs/download/dp1480.pdf (accessed 2 Feb. 2026).
5 Here defined as members of the OECD.
6 OECD, *Under Pressure: The Squeezed Middle Class* (OECD Publishing, Paris, 2019): author calculations.
7 Tony Blair Institute and Deltapoll, 'Disruptive Delivery and the Populist Challenge: What Voters Want and Why the Centre Must Change', Jan. 2025, p. 12.
8 Faster Horses, 'Decoding Populism: Uncovering Britain's Epidemic of Discontent – An Ethnographic Exploration' (Summary Report) (2025), United Kingdom.
9 £30,000–34,000 as opposed to the national median of £35,000–39,000.
10 Prof. Jane Green et al. 'The Mid-Life Economic Crisis: Addressing Voter Insecurity and Political Volatility' (2025), Joseph Rowntree Foundation.
11 Compared to only 28 per cent of 18–34-year-olds.
12 Green et al. 'The Mid-Life Economic Crisis: Addressing Voter Insecurity and Political Volatility' (2025), Joseph Rowntree Foundation, found that income deciles alone are poor predictors of economic insecurity. In fact,

NOTES

over 23 per cent of those in the top two income deciles still report high economic insecurity, and many in the lowest income bands do not.
13 Ibid. p. 51.
14 Will Marshall, Deborah Mattinson and Claire Ainsley, 'PPI 2024 Election Review and the Way Ahead for Democrats' (Washington, DC: Progressive Policy Institute, Dec. 2024), p. 3.
15 OECD, 'Low-Wage Employment in France' (Jan. 2025), available at https://www.oecd.org/en/publications/2025/01/low-wage-employment-in-france_ac641c84.html (accessed 2 Feb. 2026).
16 OECD, 'OECD Economic Surveys: Italy 2019' (Apr. 2019), available at https://www.oecd.org/en/publications/2019/04/oecd-economic-surveys-italy-2019_25adf6f1.html (accessed 2 Feb. 2026).
17 Deborah Mattinson, Claire Ainsley and Tom Brookes, 'Build Back Belief: Why Voters Around the World Lost Faith in Government and How to Win It Back' (Washington, DC: Progressive Policy Institute, Jul. 2025).
18 Pew Research Center, '7 Facts About Germany's AfD Party', 20 Sep. 2024, available at www.pewresearch.org/short-reads/2024/09/20/7-facts-about-germanys-afd-party/ (accessed 2 Feb. 2026).
19 This sense was confirmed by the excellent work of the Independent Commission on Neighbourhoods (ICON), which found that people define their neighbourhoods at a strikingly small scale: not towns or districts, but estates, cul-de-sacs, and even a handful of streets. See Independent Commission on Neighbourhoods, Public First, 'Neighbourhood Decline and Populist Resentment: Insights from the ICON Research Report' (2025).
20 David R. K. Adler and Ben W. Ansell, 'Housing and Populism', *West European Politics* 43 (2) (2020): pp. 344–65, https://doi.org/10.1080/01402382.2019.1615322
21 Brookings Institution, 'Trump again won counties representing a minority share of national GDP – but with notable gains (updated 19 Dec. 2024), available at: www.brookings.edu/articles/trump-again-won-counties-representing-a-minority-share-of-national-gdp-but-with-notable-gains (accessed 2 Feb. 2026).
22 W. A. Galston and E. C. Kamarck, 'Renewing the Democratic Party' (Third Way, 2 Feb. 2025), available at https://www.thirdway.org/report/renewing-the-democratic-party (accessed 2 Feb. 2026).
23 David Adler and Ben Ansell, 'Housing and Populism' in *Bricks in the Wall: The Politics of Housing in Europe*, published online 7 Jun. 2019, pp. 344–65.
24 Cited Joel Suss, 'Beware populist economics: History suggests the political approach ends in unsustainable debt and lower GDP', *Financial Times*, 24 Aug. 2025.

25 See Andrés Rodríguez-Pose, Javier Terrero-Dávila and Neil Lee, 'Left-behind versus unequal places: interpersonal inequality, economic decline and the rise of populism in the USA and Europe', *Journal of Economic Geography* 23, no. 5 (Sep. 2023), pp. 951–77.
26 Social Market Foundation (SMF).
27 I defined this as 30 per cent vote at the general election, which is around twice the national average Reform vote once we exclude Scotland and Northern Ireland.
28 You can find detailed analysis at https://liambyrnemp.substack.com/p/rage-to-riches (accessed 2 Feb. 2026).
29 See Best for Britain/YouGov, 'Decoding Populism: Who Are Reform UK's Voters?' (summary report), London: Best for Britain, 8 Aug. 2025. Sixty-two per cent of Reform-minded voters said that their area had declined compared to 48 per cent of all voters.
30 Which we define here as the segment Disgusted Disruptors.
31 Independent Commission on Neighbourhoods (ICON), Public First, 'Neighbourhood Decline and Populist Resentment: Insights from the ICON Research Report' (2025).
32 'Higher levels of crime …', it found, 'was another feature that the model identified as corresponding to higher levels of Reform vote share'. See SMF.
33 As they reported, 'They're living in estates where there's nothing to do … You've got young people selling drugs. The other half want to be famous. Nobody wants to learn a trade' (woman, 30s, West Bromwich). See ICON, Public First, 'Neighbourhood Decline and Populist Resentment: Insights from the ICON Research Report' (2025).
34 Ibid.
35 Tony Blair Institute and Deltapoll, 'Disruptive Delivery and the Populist Challenge: What Voters Want and Why the Centre Must Change', Jan. 2025, p. 12.
36 Arlie Russell Hochschild, *Strangers in Their Own Land: Anger and Mourning on the American Right* (The New Press, 2018, Kindle edition), Location 2351.
37 Best for Britain/YouGov, 'Decoding Populism: Who Are Reform UK's Voters?' (summary report), London: Best for Britain, 8 Aug. 2025.
38 Quoted Will Marshall, Deborah Mattinson and Claire Ainsley, '2024 Election Review and the Way Ahead for Democrats' (Washington, DC: Progressive Policy Institute, Dec. 2024).
39 Tony Blair Institute for Global Change, 'Elections Explained: Rise of the AfD Signals a New Era for Germany' (July 2024), available at https://

institute.global/insights/geopolitics-and-security/elections-explained-rise-of-the-afd-signals-a-new-era-for-germany (accessed 2 Feb. 2026)
40 W. A. Galston and E. C. Kamarck, 'Renewing the Democratic Party' (Third Way, 2 Feb. 2025), available at www.thirdway.org/report/renewing-the-democratic-party (accessed 2 Feb. 2026).
41 Will Marshall, Deborah Mattinson and Claire Ainsley, '2024 Election Review and the Way Ahead for Democrats' (Washington, DC: Progressive Policy Institute, Dec. 2024).
42 Ibid.
43 Tesler, Michael. 'How immigration swung voters of color to Trump', 538, 20 Nov. 2024, https://abcnews.go.com/538/immigration-swung-voters-color-trump/story?id=116016407 (accessed 2 Feb. 2026).
44 Bréville, Benoît. 'How voting for Le Pen stopped being shameful', Le Monde diplomatique, available at https://mondediplo.com/2025/03/03rassemblement-national (accessed 2 Feb. 2026).
45 Will Marshall, Deborah Mattinson and Claire Ainsley, '2024 Election Review and the Way Ahead for Democrats' (Washington, DC: Progressive Policy Institute, Dec. 2024).
46 British Future, forthcoming. See for updates.
47 Peter wrote up his superb remarks at https://kellnerp.substack.com/p/how-to-defeat-populism (accessed 2 Feb. 2026).
48 Quoted Edward Fishman, *Chokepoints: American Power in the Age of Economic Warfare* (New York: Penguin Random House, 2025), p. 5.
49 The IMF now warns that global debt could climb to 117 per cent of GDP by 2027, a level not seen since the Second World War. See *International Monetary Fund, Fiscal Monitor – April 2025: Fiscal Policy under Uncertainty* (Washington, DC: IMF, 2025), Chapter 1: Fiscal Policy under Uncertainty, figure 1.14, panel 1, indicates that global debt-at-risk is estimated at about 117 percent of GDP for 2027.
50 *Economist*, 'Fear the Deficit-Populism Doom Loop', 23 Aug. 2025.
51 You can find Kelly's slides at www.ipsos.com/sites/default/files/ct/publication/documents/2025-02/2024-what happened_Kelly Beaver_v3.pdf (accessed 2 Feb. 2026).
52 Will Marshall, Deborah Mattinson and Claire Ainsley, '2024 Election Review and the Way Ahead for Democrats' (Washington, DC: Progressive Policy Institute, Dec. 2024), p. 7.
53 Tony Blair Institute, 'Disruptive Delivery: Meeting the Unmet Demand in Politics', 30 Jan. 2025.

NOTES

54 Fondation pour l'innovation politique (Fondapol), 'AfD: the German Far Right at a Dead End' (Jun. 2024), available at www.fondapol.org/en/study/afd-the-german-far-right-at-a-dead-end (accessed 2 Feb. 2026).

55 Will Marshall, Deborah Mattinson and Claire Ainsley, '2024 Election Review and the Way Ahead for Democrats' (Washington, DC: Progressive Policy Institute, Dec. 2024).

4 What's the Message?

1 K. A. Hawkins, R. Aguilar, B. Castanho Silva, E. K. Jenne, B. Kocijan and C. Rovira Kaltwasser, 'Measuring Populist Discourse: The Global Populism Database', paper presented at the 2019 EPSA Annual Conference in Belfast, UK, 20–22 Jun.

2 I am grateful to Ben Byrne for his advice on the semiotics of all this.

3 Further examples include the Swedish Democrats' 'Keep Sweden Swedish'; or Viktor Orban's 'keep Hungary Hungarian'.

4 Specifically, we used two techniques. First, a Latent Semantic Analysis (LSA), which is a method of textual analysis that groups together words based on co-occurrence. The output of this analysis is patterns of topics or themes characterised by the frequency with which particular terms or words appear together, or 'co-occur'. In short, if a selection of words appears together, in close proximity across many speeches, the LSA will group them together, implying a theme. Second, we used Topic Clustering (sometimes known as Semantic Clustering), a technique that groups frequently used words together by their semantic similarity. These different clusters light up the rhetorical features of a speech; they are the typical style, the framing, character or narrative features of a speech. If words, like those relating to 'time' for example, are frequently included, we might infer something about a series of speeches, such as 'temporal framing'.

5 Richard Tice, speech at Reform UK Regional Party Conference in Doncaster, 2024.

6 Fyodor Dostoevsky, *The Brothers Karamazov*, Book III, Chapter 3.

7 'There's a kernel of truth in everything Trump says', as the Ambassador [Peter Mandelson] put it, *The Times*, 20 Jul. 2024, available at www.thetimes.com/uk/politics/article/peter-mandelson-theres-a-kernel-of-truth-in-everything-trump-says-jhlbphh6g (accessed 2 Feb. 2026).

NOTES

8   Donald Trump, speech to Joint Session of Congress in 2017.
9   Andrea Jenkyns, Greater Lincolnshire mayoralty victory speech, 2025.
10 Sam Bowles and Herb Gintis put it like this: 'groups with more altruists survive challenges, encroaching on less cooperative groups or even eliminating them' in *A Cooperative Species: Human Reciprocity and Its Evolution* (Princeton, 2011), p. 103.
11 See Charles Darwin, *The Descent of Man* (Prometheus Books, 1998).
12 Ibid.
13 D. S. Wilson, *This View of Life: Completing the Darwinian Revolution* (Alfred Knopf, 2019), p. 91. As Wilson puts it: 'Almost everything that sets us apart from other primate species can be explained as forms of cooperation that evolved by between-group selection, thanks largely to our ability to suppress disruptive within-group selection'.
14 Yuval Noah Harari, *Sapiens: A Brief History of Humankind* (London: Penguin, 2011), p. 352.
15 Donald Trump making presidential candidate announcement, 2015.
16 Nigel Farage, party manifesto launch, 2024.
17 Nigel Farage, announcement of standing for election, 2024.
18 Viktor Orbán, party conference, 2024.
19 Oswald Spengler, *The Decline of the West* (Volumes I & II), translated by Charles Francis Atkinson, (Alfred A. Knopf, 1926–8). Originally published in German as *Der Untergang des Abendlandes*, 1918–22.
20 Ibid. Vol. 1: *Form and Actuality*.
21 See Mark Sedgwick, *Key Thinkers of the Radical Right: Behind the New Threat to Liberal Democracy* (Oxford University Press, 2019).
22 An idea known as meta-politics, derived from the work of Italian Marxist Antonio Gramsci. See Antonio Gramsci, *Selections from the Prison Notebooks*, edited and translated by Quintin Hoare and Geoffrey Nowell Smith (Lawrence & Wishart, 1971), in particular the concepts of cultural hegemony, war of position, and the work of organic intellectuals.
23 Renaud Camus, *Le Grand Remplacement* (Éditions David Reinharc, 2011), p.16.
24 David Engels, 'Oswald Spengler and the Decline of the West' in *Key Thinkers of the Radical Right: Behind the New Threat to Liberal Democracy*, edited by Mark Sedgwick (Oxford University Press, 2019).
25 Jean Raspail, *Le Camp des Saints* [*The Camp of the Saints*] (Éditions Robert Laffont, Paris, 1973), English translation by Norman R. Shapiro (Charles Scribner's Sons, New York, 1975).
26 Renaud Camus, Le Grand Remplacement (Éditions David Reinharc, 2011).

NOTES

27 Michel Houellebecq, Submission, translated by Lorin Stein (Farrar, Straus and Giroux, 2015), originally published in French as Soumission (Flammarion, 2015).
28 Or as Zemmour puts it in *The Suicide of France*, 'The feminisation of society is the emasculation of the nation'.
29 See Elian Peltier and Nicholas Kulish, 'A Racist Book's Malign and Lingering Influence', *New York Times*, 22 Nov. 2019. And 'The world of Marine le Pen is somewhere between George Orwell and Michel Houellebecq', concludes writer Michel Eltchaninoff in *Inside the Mind of Marine Le Pen* (Hurst & Co., 2018).
30 Barring Enoch Powell, of course, whose 'rivers of blood' speech sparked outrage in 1968.
31 See, for instance, Douglas Murray, *The Strange Death of Europe: Immigration, Identity, Islam* (Bloomsbury Continuum, 2017); Douglas Murray, *The War on the West* (HarperCollins, 2022); Christopher Caldwell, *Reflections on the Revolution in Europe: Immigration, Islam and the West* (Allen Lane, 2009); David Goodhart, *The Road to Somewhere: The Populist Revolt and the Future of Politics* (C. Hurst & Co., 2017).
32 Christopher Caldwell, *Europe, Reflections on the Revolution in Europe: Immigration, Islam and the West* (2009).
33 Ibid.
34 Ibid. p. 286.
35 Ibid. p. 270.
36 Murray, ibid. p. 7.
37 Ibid. p. 8.
38 In short, paleoconservatives emphasise tradition, national sovereignty, cultural homogeneity, and non-interventionist foreign policy. They are sceptical of globalism, immigration and liberal democracy. In contrast, neoconservatives advocate for free markets, liberal internationalism, and an activist foreign policy, especially the promotion of democracy abroad. The division between the two became sharpest around the invasion of Iraq. Where paleoconservatives defend national identity and hierarchy, neoconservatives champion a universalist vision of American values. See Francis Fukuyama, *America at the Crossroads: Democracy, Power, and the Neoconservative Legacy* (Yale University Press, 2006).
39 See Edward Ashbee, 'Patrick J. Buchanan and the Death of the West' in Mark Sedgwick (ed.), *Key Thinkers of the Radical Right: Behind the New Threat to Liberal Democracy* (Oxford University Press, 2019), p.126.
40 Pat Buchanan, *The Death of the West* (2001), Afterword.
41 Ibid. p. 13.

42 Ibid. p. 181.
43 Douglas Murray, *The Strange Death of Europe: Immigration, Identity, Islam* (Bloomsbury Continuum, 4 May 2017). The book opens with his declaration that 'Europe is committing suicide'.
44 Renaud Camus, *Le Grand Remplacement* (Éditions David Reinharc, 2011), p. 51.
45 Pat Buchanan, *The Death of the West* (2001), p. 23.
46 Geert Wilders, speech to think tank, 2008.
47 Viktor Orbán, speech to party conference, 2015.
48 Marine Le Pen, speech to party conference, 2018.
49 Nigel Farage, speech to party conference, 2024.
50 Ezra Klein, *Why We're Polarized* (Profile, 2020), Kindle edn.
51 Drew Western, *The Political Brain: The Role of Emotion in Deciding the Fate of the Nation* (PublicAffairs, 2008).

5 Magical Thinking

1 Edmund Burke, *Reflections on the Revolution in France*, 1790.
2 Joseph de Maistre, *Essai sur le principe générateur des constitutions politiques; suivi de Étude sur la souveraineté* (1884); 'Les hommes ne respectent jamais ce qu'ils ont fait'.
3 Alexis de Tocquville, *Democracy in America*, Vol. I.
4 G. K. Chesterton, *The Drift from Domesticity*, 1929.
5 Michael Oakeshot, 'On Being Conservative', 1956.
6 Russell Kirk, 'Ten Conservative Principles'.
7 Roger Scruton, *How to Be a Conservative*, 2014.
8 France 24, '"Mother, Italian, Christian": Giorgia Meloni, Italy's far-right leader on the cusp of power', 24 Sep. 2022, available at https://www.france24.com/en/europe/20220924-mother-italian-christian-giorgia-meloni-italy-s-far-right-leader-on-the-cusp-of-power (accessed 2 Feb. 2026).
9 Giorgia Meloni, program speech, 2022.
10 Giorgio Meloni, keynote address at the Conservative Political Action Conference, 2025.
11 Donald Trump, Florida keynote speech, 21 April 2022.
12 Nigel Farage, party conference speech, 2013.
13 Viktor Orbán, party conference speech, 2017.
14 Patrick J. Deneen, *Why Liberalism Failed* (New Haven, CT: Yale University Press, 2018).
15 Ibid. p. x.

16 Ibid. p. 3.
17 As Deneen puts it, 'the loosening of social bonds in nearly every aspect of life – familial, neighborly, communal, religious, even national – reflects the advancing logic of liberalism and is the source of its deepest instability'. Ibid. p. 30.
18 Ibid. p. 39.
19 Ibid. p. 41.
20 A truth that economist Thomas Philippon confirmed, in his famous book *The Great Reversal*, was largely explained by a corruption of politics: 'Competition has declined in most sectors of the US economy [but] ... The lack of competition is explained largely by policy choices influenced by lobbying and campaign finance contributions.' See T. Philippon, *The Great Reversal: How America Gave Up on Free Markets* (Cambridge, MA: Belknap Press of Harvard University Press, 2019).
21 Christopher Caldwell, *Europe, Reflections on the Revolution in Europe: Immigration, Islam and the West* (2009), p. 270.
22 Ibid. p. 270.
23 Giorgia Meloni, program speech, 2022.
24 Marine Le Pen, party conference, 2018.
25 Richard Tice, party conference, 2023.
26 For a survey of the techno-libertarian's intellectual influences, see S. Freedman, 'Technology vs Democracy: The origins and ideology of Muskworld', Comment is Freed (Substack), 12 Feb. 2025, retrieved from https://samf.substack.com/p/technology-vs-democracy; also I. Ward, 'The seven intellectual forces behind JD Vance's worldview', *Politico* magazine, 18 Jul. 2024 from and J. Pogue, 'Inside the New Right, Where Peter Thiel Is Placing His Biggest Bets', *Vanity Fair*, 20 Apr. 2022 from https://www.vanityfair.com/news/2022/04/inside-the-new-right-where-peter-thiel-is-placing-his-biggest-bets?srsltid=AfmBOootBjQjdol2YeXy4YgYnMrNa1LWUYK0ApZrs3-sPgmsrPLWRxzk (accessed 2 Feb. 2026).
27 Joshua Tait, 'Mencius Moldbug and Neoreaction' in Mark Sedgwick (ed.) *Key Thinkers of the Radical Right: Behind the New Threat to Liberal Democracy*, (Oxford University Press, 2019).
28 N. Stephenson, *Snow Crash* (New York, NY: Bantam Books, 1992).
29 C. Pein, 'Mouthbreathing Machiavellis Dream of a Silicon Reich', *The Baffler*, 19 May 2014, retrieved from *The Baffler* website.
30 Hans-Hermann Hoppe, *Democracy: The God That Failed: The Economics and Politics of Monarchy, Democracy, and Natural Order* (New Brunswick, NJ: Transaction Publishers, 2001).
31 Peter Thiel, 'The Education of a Libertarian', Cato Unbound, Apr. 2009.

6 Engage and Enrage

1. The earliest source for these immortal words is supplied by Cicero in *De Oratore* (55 BCE), Book III, 213–14. Cicero recalls a story told about Demosthenes: 'When asked what was the first part of oratory, Demosthenes replied, "Delivery." When asked the second, he replied, "Delivery." When asked the third, he replied again, "Delivery." Quintilian later repeats the anecdote in *Institutio Oratoria* (Book XI, ch. 3).
2. L. Graves, 'For the first time, social media overtakes TV as Americans' top news source', Nieman Lab, 17 Jun. 2005, available at www.niemanlab.org/2025/06/for-the-first-time-social-media-overtakes-tv-as-americans-top-news-source/ (accessed 2 Feb. 2026).
3. European Parliament (2023), 'TV still main source for news but social media is gaining ground' [online], available at https://www.europarl.europa.eu/news/en/press-room/20231115IPR11303/tv-still-main-source-for-news-but-social-media-is-gaining-ground (accessed 2 Feb. 2026).
4. S. Feldman and K. Stenner, 'Perceived Threat and Authoritarianism', *Political Pyschology*, Vol. 18, No. 4, 1997, quoted in Moises Naim, *The Revenge of Power*, p. 99.
5. T. Wu, *The Attention Merchants: The Epic Scramble to Get Inside Our Heads* (New York: Knopf, 2016).
6. Ibid. p. 5.
7. Ibid. p. 6.
8. Science, Innovation and Technology Committee, 'Social Media, Misinformation and Harmful Algorithms', House of Commons, UK Parliament, 2025, paragraph 79.
9. Ibid. paragraph 82.
10. For a superb guide, see Tobias Rose-Stockwell, *Outrage Machine: How Tech Amplifies Discontent, Disrupts Democracy – and What We Can Do About It* (London: Hachette UK, 2023), foreword by Jonathan Haidt.
11. William J. Brady et al. 'Emotion Shapes the Diffusion of Moralized Content in Social Networks', PNAS 114, no. 28 (2017), pp. 7316–21, https://doi.org/10.1073/pnas.1618923114
12. Pew Research Center, 'How the public reacted on Facebook', 23 Feb. 2017.
13. Soroush Vosoughi, Deb Roy and Sinan Aral, 'The spread of true and false news online', Science 359, no. 6380 (2018), pp. 1146–51, https://doi.org/10.1126/science.aap9559

NOTES

14 Sinan Aral, *The Hype Machine: How Social Media Disrupts Our Elections, Our Economy, and Our Health – and How We Must Adapt* (New York: Currency, 2020).
15 Peter Dizikes, 'Why Social Media Has Changed the World – and How to Fix It', *MIT News*, 24 Sep. 2020.
16 Aristotle, *Rhetoric*, translated by W. Rhys Roberts (New York: Modern Library, 1954).
17 Antonio Gramsci, *Selections from the Prison Notebooks of Antonio Gramsci*, ed. Quintin Hoare and Geoffrey Nowell Smith (New York: International Publishers, 1971).
18 Quoted Nathan Sperber and George Hoare, 'How the Right Hijacked Antonio Gramsci', *Jacobin*, 15 Mar. 2025.
19 Ibid.
20 Rita Abrahamsen, Jean-François Drolet, Michael C. Williams, Srdjan Vucetić, Karin Narita and Alexandra Gheciu, 'The Gramscian Right, or Turning Gramsci on His Head' in *World of the Right: Radical Conservatism and Global Order* (Cambridge: Cambridge University Press, 2024), pp. 34–66. https://doi.org/10.1017/9781009516075.002. p. 47
21 Pat Buchanan, *The Death of the West* (2001), p. 77.
22 Quoted, Abrahamsen et al. 'The Gramscian Right, or Turning Gramsci on His Head' in World of the Right: Radical Conservatism and Global Order (Cambridge: Cambridge University Press, 2024), p. 62.
23 John Ganz, *When the Clock Broke: Con Men, Conspiracists, and How America Cracked Up in the Early 1990s* (New York: Farrar, Straus and Giroux, 2024), p. 100.
24 See J. Philipp Thomeczek, 'Political communication on Facebook: do populist parties send out more posts?' Party Politics 30, no. 6 (2024), pp. 1143–51, https://doi.org/10.1177/13540688231184626
25 See Clara Hendrickson and William A. Galston, 'Why are populists winning online? Social media reinforces their anti-establishment message', Brookings, available at www.brookings.edu/articles/why-are-populists-winning-online-social-media-reinforces-their-anti-establishment-message/ (accessed 2 Feb. 2026).
26 Written evidence submitted by Hossein Dabbagh, Northeastern University London and Oxford University to the JCNSS Inquiry on Defending Democracy: 'Algorithmic Echoes: Social Media, Polarisation and the Surge of Extremism in British Democracy' (2024).
27 Ferenc Huszár, Sofia I. Ktena, Conor O'Brien, Luca Belli, Áine Schlaikjer and Moritz Hardt, 'Algorithmic Amplification of Politics on Twitter', arXiv (2021), https://arxiv.org/abs/2110.11010 (accessed 2 Feb. 2026).

28 Adam Satariano, 'TikTok Pushed Young German Voters toward Far-Right Party, Study Finds', *Wired*, 22 May 2024, www.wired.com/story/TikTok-german-voters-afd/ (accessed 2 Feb. 2026).
29 Global Witness, 'X and TikTok algorithms push pro-AfD content to non-partisan German users: new analysis', 20 Feb. 2025.
30 I am immensely grateful to my fellow Parliamentary Fellow for the programme, Rt Hon. John Glen MP for hosting this programme with me: Policy-Making in the Age of Populism.
31 By Maggie Haberman, Glenn Thrush and Peter Baker, 'Inside Trump's Hour-by-Hour Battle for Self-Preservation', *New York Times*, 9 Dec. 2017.
32 Nic Newman et al., Reuters Institute, 'Digital News Report 2024' (Oxford: Reuters Institute for the Study of Journalism, Jun. 2024).
33 See Christopher Paul and Miriam Matthews, 'The Russian "Firehose of Falsehood" Propaganda Model: Why It Might Work and Options to Counter It', PE-198. Santa Monica, CA: RAND Corporation (2016), www.rand.org/pubs/perspectives/PE198.html (accessed 2 Feb. 2026).
34 Cambridge Disinformation Summit (2025), www.jbs.cam.ac.uk/events/cambridge-disinformation-summit-2025/ (accessed 2 Feb. 2026).
35 David Roberts, 'Donald Trump and the Rise of Tribal Epistemology', *Vox*, 22 Mar. 2017.
36 Science, Innovation and Technology Committee, 'Social Media, Misinformation and Harmful Algorithms', House of Commons, UK Parliament, Summary (2025).
37 We found the breakdown of primary news sources as follows: social-media networks (12 per cent), a news app on a device (11 per cent), a news website (9 per cent) or a newspaper website (8 per cent). A good old-fashioned printed paper was a long way behind. Just 4 per cent of Reform-curious voters read a daily paper.

7 Follow the Money

1 See Liam Byrne, *Dragons: Ten Entrepreneurs Who Built Britain* (London: Head of Zeus, 2016).
2 Spotlight on Corruption, 'How Malign and Foreign Donations Could Hijack the Next UK General Election' (London, 2024).
3 Transparency International UK (2025). 'New research reveals almost £1 in every £10 of political donations comes from "unknown or questionable sources"', available at www.transparency.org.uk/news/new-research-reveals-almost-ps1-every-ps10-political-donations-comes-unknown-or-questionable (accessed 22 Aug. 2025).

NOTES

4. RUSI (2025), 'Democracy's weakest link: foreign money and political influence', London: Royal United Services Institute. Quoted in submission to the Joint Committee on the National Security Strategy: 'there are well-identified loopholes that allow for the possibility of donations from overseas sources to enter the UK political funding system' (Joint Committee, 2025).
5. Peter Geoghegan, 'Making Media Great Again', *London Review of Books*, 47(4) (2025), pp. 25–7, available at https://www.lrb.co.uk/the-paper/v47/n04/peter-geoghegan/making-media-great-again (accessed 22 Aug. 2025).
6. Cited, Andrew Graystone, 'The Marshall Plan: Paul Marshall and GB News', *Prospect* magazine, 17 May 2025, available at https://www.prospectmagazine.co.uk/ideas/media/65415/the-marshall-plan-paul-marshall-gb-news (accessed 22 Aug. 2025).
7. Hope not hate, 'Revealed: The Shocking Tweets of GB News Co-owner Sir Paul Marshall', Hope not hate, 22 Feb. 2024, available at https://hopenothate.org.uk/2024/02/22/revealed-the-shocking-tweets-of-gb-news-co-owner-sir-paul-marshall/ (accessed 22 Aug. 2025).
8. George Parker and Daniel Thomas, 'How GB News became the pulpit of right wing politics in Britain', *Financial Times*, 23 Mar. 2024. Available https://www.ft.com/content/e2f6e6fe-5451-45ec-95f6-dcdb4f511114 (Accessed: 22 August 2025).
9. Anna Gross, 'Nigel Farage's media company records £1.25mn profit', *Financial Times*, 26 Feb. 2025, www.ft.com/content/42c5f8ed-9c93-4158-a3da-22ea6feb6a65
10. Cat Zakrzewski and David Shepardson, 'Elon Musk's voter sweepstakes faces federal court challenge', *Washington Post*, 31 Oct. 2024, available at https://www.washingtonpost.com/technology/2024/10/31/elon-musk-voter-sweepstakes-federal-court/ (accessed 22 Aug. 2025).
11. Rebecca Ballhaus and Shawn Boburg, 'Trump Organization Plots Expansion as Trump Returns to Power', *Wall Street Journal*, 19 Jan. 2025, available at www.wsj.com/politics/policy/trump-organization-expansion-4998172b (accessed: 22 Aug. 2025).
12. Anne Applebaum, *Autocracy Inc.: The Dictators Who Want to Run the World*, Kindle edn (London: Penguin Books, 2024), p. 2.
13. Jan-Werner Müller, 'Trump's Corruption Is in a League of Its Own', Project Syndicate, 3 Jun. 2025, available at https://www.project-syndicate.org/commentary/trump-corruption-leage-of-its-own-by-jan-werner-mueller-2025-06 (accessed 22 Aug. 2025).
14. Demetri Sevastopulo, 'Trump earned $57mn from crypto venture, disclosure shows', *Financial Times*, 15 May 2025, available at www.ft.com/content/1508d831-60bb-4287-9c76-da7d730cf584 (accessed: 22 Aug. 2025).

NOTES

15 CBS News, 'Trump family's net worth bolstered by cryptocurrency investments', CBS News, 16 May 2025, available at https://www.cbsnews.com/news/trump-family-net-worth-crypto-investments/ (accessed 22 Aug.2025).
16 David D. Kirkpatrick, 'The Number: How Much Is Trump Pocketing Off the Presidency?' *New Yorker*, 11 Aug. 2025.
17 Ibid.
18 BBC News, 'Reform UK to accept Bitcoin donations, says Farage', 30 May 2025, available at www.bbc.co.uk/news/articles/cg4vnd0d17r0 (accessed 2 Feb. 2026).
19 Protos (14 Oct. 2021), 'The Tether Papers: Investigation into the USDT stablecoin', https://protos.com/tether-papers-crypto-stablecoin-usdt-investigation-analysis/ (accessed 2 Feb. 2026).
20 R. Booth and P. Geoghegan (23 May 2024), 'George Cottrell, Nigel Farage, and Reform's links to Geostrategy International and unlimited company donations', openDemocracy.
21 See Intelligence and Security Committee of Parliament, 'Russia: Report', London: UK Parliament, 21 Jul. 2020, https://isc.independent.gov.uk/wp-content/uploads/2021/01/CCS207_CCS0520958920-001_ISC_Russia_Report_web_accessible.pdf (accessed 2 Feb. 2026).
22 Senate Committee on Foreign Relations, 'Putin's Asymmetric Assault on Democracy in Russia and Europe: Implications for U.S. National Security', Committee Print No. 115–21 (Washington, DC: US Government Publishing Office, 10 Jan. 2018).
23 For a good summary, see Alina Polyakova, Marlene Laruelle, Stefan Meister and Neil Barnett, 'The Kremlin's Trojan Horses: Russian Influence in France, Germany, and the United Kingdom', Washington, DC: Atlantic Council, Dinu Patriciu Eurasia Center, Nov. 2016,
24 Edward Wong and Julian E. Barnes, 'Russia Secretly Gave $300 Million to Political Parties and Officials Worldwide, U.S. Says', *New York Times*, 13 Sep. 2022,
25 Paul Sonne, 'A Russian bank gave Marine Le Pen's party a loan. Then weird things began happening', *Washington Post*, 27 Dec. 2018.
26 Reuters, 'Changing Tune, Italy's Salvini Pledges to Help Refugees from Ukraine', 8 Mar. 2022.
27 *Der Spiegel*, 'How the AfD Became the Long Arm of Russia and China', 1 May 2024, available at www.spiegel.de/international/germany/afd-spionageaffaere-russland-und-china-im-fokus-neue-enthuellungen-belasten-die-partei-1714480876-a-a1c05e64-b6bc-4c6b-844e-a78a32ec4f91?utm_source=chatgpt.com (accessed 2 Feb. 2026).

28 Centre for Information Resilience (Jun. 2025), 'A7A5: Circumventing sanctions with stablecoin cryptocurrency', London, www.info-res.org/app/uploads/2025/06/A7A5-Report-June-2025-Final-Draft-1.pdf (accessed 2 Feb. 2026).
29 Adam Sage, 'The "French Elon Musk" bankrolling the country's populist right', *The Times*, 8 Aug. 2025.

Conclusion

1 Deborah Mattinson, 'Kamala Harris's Policies Target "Hero Voters" in Swing States', *The Times*, 6 Sep. 2024.
2 Edward Fieldhouse, Jane Green, Geoffrey Evans, Jonathan Mellon, Christopher Prosser, Hermann Schmitt and Cees van der Eijk, *Electoral Shocks: The Volatile Voter in a Turbulent World* (Oxford: Oxford University Press, 2020).
3 John Maynard Keynes, 'Economic Possibilities for Our Grandchildren' in *Essays in Persuasion* (London: Macmillan, 1931), pp. 358–73.
4 As such, Gordon argues, fast economic growth could prove a one-time thing centred on 1750–2050 and may now tail off below 0.5 per cent a year. See R. J. Gordon, 'Is U.S. Economic Growth Over? Faltering Innovation Confronts the Six Headwinds', NBER Working Paper No. 18315, Centre for Economic Policy Research Policy Insight No. 63, Sep. 2012.
5 K. Georgieva, 'The Economic Possibilities for My Grandchildren' [keynote speech delivered at King's College, Cambridge, UK (14 Mar. 2024)], International Monetary Fund, retrieved from https://www.imf.org/en/news/articles/2024/03/08/sp031424-kings-college-cambridge-kristalina-georgieva (accessed 2 Feb. 2026).
6 While the exact share varies by region and by how SME is defined, broadly speaking small and medium-sized enterprises are responsible for somewhere between 45 and 65 per cent of employment in developed economies.
7 Reducing energy bills was prioritised by 73 per cent; raising the personal tax-free allowance, by 69 per cent; and cutting income tax, by 55 per cent. In contrast, only small minorities prioritised traditional welfare measures such as council-tax support (12 per cent) or social care (10 per cent).
8 International Monetary Fund, 'United Kingdom: Selected Issues', IMF Staff Country Report No. 25/205, European Department, 25 Jul. 2025, doi:10.5089/9798229018746.002
9 See Gaëll Mainguy, Marie-Cécile Naves and François Taddei, 'Building a Learning and Sustainable Planet Together' in *The Future of Work for the*

People We Serve, ed. Liam Byrne MP (Paris: The Parliamentary Network on the World Bank and International Monetary Fund, 2018), pp. 87–93.
10 A phrase I owe to former Cabinet minister Rt Hon. John Denham. See John Denham (19 Jun. 2004), 'The fairness code', *Prospect magazine*, accessed from https://www.prospectmagazine.co.uk/essays/59007/the-fairness-code (accessed 2 Feb. 2026).
11 Hayek went as far as to condemn 'social justice' as being as meaningless as to speak of a 'moral stone' – see F. Hayek, *Law, Legislation and Liberty: The Mirage of Social Justice* (University of Chicago, 1976), Vol. 2, p. 78.
12 As Samuel Bowles and Herbert Gintis, developing the work of Robert Axelrod and others, once put it: 'The welfare state is in trouble not because selfishness is rampant (it is not) but because many egalitarian programmes no longer evoke, and sometimes now offend, deeply held notions of fairness, encompassing both reciprocity and generosity, but stopping far short of unconditional altruism towards the less well off.'
13 A nuance I owe to Peter Hyman.
14 William A. Galston, *Anger, Fear, Domination: Dark Passions and the Power of Political Speech* (New Haven: Yale University Press, 2024).
15 O. Haynes, 'Tommy Robinson's "Unite the Kingdom" rally was sponsored by a convicted fraudster allegedly behind cryptocurrency "rug pulls"', *Byline Times*, 1 Oct. 2025, available at https://bylinetimes.com/2025/10/01/tommy-robinsons-unite-the-kingdom-rally-was-sponsored-by-a-convicted-fraudster-allegedly-behind-cryptocurrency-rug-pulls/ (accessed 2 Feb. 2026).
16 Sunder Katwala, *How to Be a Patriot: Why Love of Country Can End Our Very British Culture War* (HarperCollins, 2023).
17 Sidney Blumenthal, *The Permanent Campaign: Inside the World of Elite Political Operatives* (Boston: Beacon Press, 1980).

About the Author

The Rt Hon Liam Byrne MP is a British Labour Party politician and the MP for Birmingham Hodge Hill and Solihull North. He is a member of His Majesty's Privy Council and the Chair of the House of Commons Business and Trade Select Committee. He chaired the Global Parliamentary Network on the World Bank and International Monetary Fund 2019–2025. He served in the Cabinet in 10 Downing Street and Her Majesty's Treasury. An Honorary Professor of Social Science at the University of Birmingham, Liam was the 2024–2025 Visiting Parliamentary Fellow at St Antony's College, Oxford. He was a Fulbright scholar at the Harvard Business School and Gwilym Gibbon Research Fellow at Nuffield College, Oxford. Before entering politics, Liam first worked in strategic consulting and banking; in 2000, he founded a fast-growing venture-backed European technology company. He is the author of more than twenty publications on economics, foreign policy and public service reform. His book, *The Inequality of Wealth: Why it Matters and How to Fix it*, was shortlisted for the Westminster Book Awards 2024.